4

For Your Information

Reading and Vocabulary Skills
Second Edition

KAREN BLANCHARD   CHRISTINE ROOT

PEARSON
Longman

For Your Information 4, Second Edition

Pearson Education, 10 Bank Street, White Plains, NY 10606

Staff credits: The people who made up the *For Your Information 4* team, representing editorial, production, design, and manufacturing, are Rhea Banker, Wendy Campbell, Karen Davy, Gina DiLillo, Christine Edmonds, Laura Le Dréan, Linda Moser, Edith Pullman, Paula Van Ells, and Pat Wosczyk.
Cover design: MADA Design, Inc.
Text composition: ElectraGraphics, Inc.
Text font: 11/14 New Aster
Illustrator credit: p. 220 Doug Adams
Photo credits: p.1 © Tom Bible/Alamy; **p.3** Globe Photo/Richard Carpenter; **p.12** © INTERFOTO Pressebildagentur/Alamy; **p.35** © Randy Faris/Corbis; **p.37** John A. Rizzo/PhotoDisc, Inc.; **p.45** © Rick Friedman/Corbis; **p.53** © Norman Jung/zefa/Corbis; **p.65** Blend Images/SuperStock; **p.67** Ruben Guzman; **p.73** Yellow Dog Productions/Getty Images; **p.93** Allsport/Mike Powell; **p.96** © Wolfgang Rattay/Reuters/Corbis; **p.103** Time & Life Pictures/Getty Images; **p.110** © Andrew Paterson/Alamy; **p.113** Courtesy of Richard Suinn; **p.118** © Robert Harding World Imagery/Corbis; **p.119** Drawing by Chas.Addams/The New Yorker Magazine, Inc.; **p.125** Nam Huh/AP Images; **p.143** George Grall/Getty Images; **p.157** (first) Isabella Stewart Gardner Museum, Boston; (second) AP World Wide Photos; **p.160** Isabella Stewart Gardner Museum, Boston; **p.163** © Burstein Collection/Corbis; **p.167** IT Stock Free/SuperStock; **p.173** Kevin Schafer/Getty Images; **p.174** © Stephen Frink Collection/Alamy; **p.185** Reprinted courtesy of Howard Post; **p.187** © Jay Dickman/Corbis; **p.195** © Stocktrek Images/Alamy; **p.213** Royalty-Free/Comstock Images © JupiterImages; **p.216** (first) © 1993 Robert Lorenz; (second) Courtesy of Green Seal
Text credits: See page xiv

Library of Congress Cataloging-in-Publication Data
Blanchard, Karen Lourie
  For your information / Karen Blanchard and Christine Root. — 2nd ed.
    p. cm.
  ISBN 0-13-199186-8 (1 : student book : alk. paper)—ISBN 0-13-199182-5
    (2 : student book : alk. paper)—ISBN 0-13-238008-0 (3 : student book : alk.
    paper)—ISBN 0-13-243694-9 (4 : student book : alk. paper)
  1. English language—Textbooks for foreign speakers. 2. Readers.
I. Root, Christine Baker II. Title.
PE1128.B586 2006
428.6'4—dc22   2006011193

Printed in the United States of America

4 5 6 7 8 9 10—VHG—12 11 10 09

This book is dedicated to
our sons, Daniel, Ian, and Matthew,
whose curiosity about the world keeps
them, and us, reading.

CONTENTS

Scope and Sequence

UNIT	CHAPTER	READING SELECTION	READING SKILL
1 **WHAT LANGUAGES DO YOU SPEAK?** pages 1–34	Chapter 1	Reaping the Rewards of Learning English	Reading with a Purpose Summarizing
	Chapter 2	The Hope of Esperanto	Previewing and Predicting Summarizing
	Chapter 3	Instant Messaging: Shaping Our Lives	Using Background Knowledge Skimming for the Main Idea Identifying Facts and Opinions

abcNEWS **Video Excerpt: The IM Code**

UNIT	CHAPTER	READING SELECTION	READING SKILL
2 **DON'T WORRY, BE HAPPY** pages 35–64	Chapter 1	The E-Factor!	Reading with a Purpose
	Chapter 2	Happiness Is . . .	Paraphrasing
	Chapter 3	How Color Can Change Your Life	Previewing and Predicting Making Inferences Summarizing

abcNEWS **Video Excerpt: How to Be Happy**

UNIT	CHAPTER	READING SELECTION	READING SKILL
3 **HOME AND FAMILY** pages 65–92	Chapter 1	The House on Mango Street	Making Inferences
	Chapter 2	My House	Understanding Tone
	Chapter 3	Birth Order: What It Means for Your Kids . . . and You	Using Background Knowledge Paraphrasing Using Graphic Organizers: Charts Understanding Figurative Language

abcNEWS **Video Excerpt: The Role of Birth Order in History**

UNIT	CHAPTER	READING SELECTION	READING SKILL
4 **WINNING AND LOSING** pages 93–123	Chapter 1	Athletes as Role Models	Previewing and Predicting Making Inferences Identifying Supporting Information
	Chapter 2	Olympic Marathons, Then and Now	Reading with a Purpose Scanning for Information Recognizing Sequence Using Graphic Organizers: Making a Timeline
	Chapter 3	Helping Athletes Go for the Gold	Paraphrasing Summarizing

abcNEWS **Video Excerpt: Barefoot Marathon**

VOCABULARY SKILL	APPLICATION SKILL
Learning Synonyms Understanding Word Parts: The Prefixes -*ant* and -*ent* Learning Word Forms	Reading an Autobiography Understanding Emoticons Writing a Journal Entry
Understanding Word Parts: The Suffix -*some* Understanding Word Parts: The Prefix *mis*- Learning Idioms: Expressions about Color	Reading an Interview Choosing a Title Writing a Journal Entry
Recognizing Commonly Confused Words Learning Antonyms Learning Synonyms and Antonyms	Completing a Questionnaire Writing a Journal Entry
Understanding Word Parts: The Suffixes -*ance* and -*ence* Learning Idioms: Expressions about Competition and Sports Learning Synonyms and Antonyms Understanding Word Parts: The Prefixes *en*- and *em*-	Reading Poetry Writing a Journal Entry

Scope and Sequence

UNIT	CHAPTER	READING SELECTION	READING SKILL
5 **HEALING POWER** pages 125–156	Chapter 1	Plant Power	Using Background Knowledge Taking Notes
	Chapter 2	Music's Surprising Power to Heal	Skimming for the Main Idea Identifying Supporting Information: Quoting Experts Understanding Anecdotes Summarizing
	Chapter 3	Frogs and Human Health	Skimming for the Main Idea Paraphrasing Understanding Cause and Effect

abcNEWS Video Excerpt: Matthew Savage, Jazz Pianist

UNIT	CHAPTER	READING SELECTION	READING SKILL
6 **CRIME** pages 157–184	Chapter 1	They're Stealing Our Masterpieces	Using Graphic Organizers: Charts Scanning for Information
	Chapter 2	Crime Lab	Previewing and Predicting Underlining Important Information
	Chapter 3	For Sale: Stolen Animals	Using Background Knowledge Scanning for Information Summarizing

abcNEWS Video Excerpt: Saving the Elephants

UNIT	CHAPTER	READING SELECTION	READING SKILL
7 **THE UNIVERSE AND BEYOND** pages 185–212	Chapter 1	Valuable By-Products of Space Research	Underlining Important Information
	Chapter 2	Destination Mars	Skimming for the Main Idea Identifying Facts and Opinions
	Chapter 3	Dancing to the Music of Physics	Making Inferences Understanding Comparisons

abcNEWS Video Excerpt: Rocket Men

UNIT	CHAPTER	READING SELECTION	READING SKILL
8 **BUSINESS SAVVY** pages 213–239	Chapter 1	Nothing but the Truth	Skimming for the Main Idea
	Chapter 2	Do's and Taboos	Using Background Knowledge Previewing and Predicting Taking Notes Understanding Contrast

abcNEWS Video Excerpt: Kids and Food

VOCABULARY SKILL	APPLICATION SKILL
Learning Synonyms and Antonyms **Understanding Word Parts: The Suffix** *-less* **Understanding Word Parts: The Prefix** *dis-* **Learning Homonyms**	**Reading a Prescription Label** **Writing a Journal Entry**
Learning Two-Word Verbs with *Pull* **Understanding Word Parts: The Suffix** *-ist* **Understanding Word Parts: The Prefixes** *il-, ir-, im-,* and *in-*	Taking a Survey Writing a Journal Entry
Learning Synonyms and Antonyms **Understanding Word Parts: The Suffix** *-ize* **Understanding Word Parts: The Suffixes** *-able* **and** *-ible* **Understanding Word Parts: The Suffix** *-ical*	**Researching a Planet** **Academic Degree Abbreviations** **Writing a Journal Entry**
Learning Idioms **Learning Synonyms and Antonyms** **Recognizing Commonly Confused Words**	**Analyzing Ads** **Choosing a Title** **Writing a Journal Entry**

The FYI Approach

Welcome to *For Your Information,* a reading and vocabulary-skill-building series for English-language learners. The FYI series is based on the premise that students are able to read at a higher level of English than they can produce. An important goal of the texts is to help students move beyond passive reading to become active, thoughtful, and confident readers of English.

This popular series is now in its second edition. The book numbers have changed in the new edition and include the following levels:

For Your Information 1	Beginning
For Your Information 2	High-Beginning
For Your Information 3	Intermediate
For Your Information 4	High-Intermediate

Each text in the FYI series is made up of eight thematically based units containing three chapters, which are built around high-interest reading selections with universal appeal. The levels are tailored to focus on the specific needs of students to increase their vocabulary base and build their reading skills. In addition to comprehension and vocabulary practice activities, reading and vocabulary-building skills are presented throughout each chapter. Although FYI is a reading series, students also practice speaking, listening, and writing throughout the texts. In trademark FYI style, the tasks in all books are varied, accessible, and inviting, and they provide stimuli for frequent interaction.

The Second Edition

The second edition of *For Your Information 4* features:

- new and updated reading selections
- designated target vocabulary words for study and practice
- expanded reading-skill-building activities
- vocabulary-building skills and word-attack activities
- a special focus on particular types of readings, such as poetry, ads, and short stories
- a companion DVD of ABC News excerpts on related themes, with accompanying activities
- a glossary of the target vocabulary words used in the readings

UNITS

FYI 4 contains eight units. The first seven units have three chapters, and the last, which gives students the opportunity to read a longer article, has two chapters. Every unit begins with Points to Ponder questions and concludes with a Tie It All Together section and a Vocabulary Self-Test.

Points to Ponder

These prereading questions serve to introduce the theme of each unit and activate students' background knowledge before they delve into each individual chapter.

CHAPTERS

The basic format for each chapter is as follows:

Before You Read

Each chapter opens with Before You Read, a selection of exercises designed to prime students for successful completion of the chapter. Target vocabulary words are previewed here, as are background questions, activities, and prereading skills such as Predicting and Reading with a Purpose.

As You Read

Selected chapters contain As You Read activities such as underlining important information, taking notes, and paraphrasing, which are designed to help students become active readers.

Reading

Each reading relates to the theme of the unit. For variety, the readings include articles, essays, and interviews. Close attention has been paid to the level and length of the readings, which range from 600 to 1,200 words, giving students practice in reading a longer text.

After You Read

Readings are followed by a combination of Comprehension Check questions and activities, along with Vocabulary Practice exercises that give students the opportunity to work with the target words from the reading. In addition, throughout this section, the presentation and practice of reading and vocabulary skills encourage students to develop their ability to think critically. For example, reading skills such as Identifying Supporting Information, Understanding Cause and Effect, and

Making Inferences are introduced and reinforced throughout this section. Other activities, such as paraphrasing and summarizing, prepare students to use the information they gain from reading for writing purposes. Vocabulary skills, such as Using Context Clues and Understanding Word Parts, are developed throughout. Talk It Over questions appear regularly, as do culminating activities that require students to practice real-life skills such as reading charts, organizing information into charts, taking surveys, and reading specific types of writing such as autobiographies, prescription labels, and ads.

UNIT CONCLUSION

Tie It All Together

Each unit concludes with activities that encourage students to think about, distill, and consolidate the information they have absorbed throughout the unit. Among these Tie It All Together activities are discussion questions based on the general theme of the unit, an activity that is "Just for Fun," and new activities based on an ABC News excerpt related to the unit theme. This section also features the Reader's Journal, an opportunity for students to reflect, in writing, on the ideas in each unit.

Vocabulary Self-Test

Each unit closes with a vocabulary self-test to help students review new words they've learned. Answers to the self-tests are found at the end of the book.

References

Campbell, Pat. *Teaching Reading to Adults: A Balanced Approach.* Edmonton: Grass Roots Press, 2003.

Pang, Elizabeth S., and Michael L. Kamil. *Second-Language Issues in Early Literacy and Instruction.* Stanford University: Publication Series No. 1, 2004.

Singhal, Meena. *Teaching Reading to Adult Second Language Learners: Theoretical Foundations, Pedagogical Applications, and Current Issues.* Lowell, MA: The Reading Matrix, 2005.

Text Credits

Page 3, "Reaping the Rewards of Learning English" by Jean Caldwell, *The Boston Globe*, May 30, 1994. Reprinted with the permission of Jean Caldwell and courtesy of *The Boston Globe*; **page 12**, Source: "The Hope of Esperanto" by J. D. Reed. *Time Magazine*, August 3, 1987, © 1987 Time Inc.; **page 18**, Excerpt from *Lost in Translation: A Life in a New Language* by Eva Hoffman. New York: E. P. Dutton, 1989; **page 20**, "The Snappy Lingo of Instant Messages" by Emily Sohn, reprinted with permission from *SCIENCE NEWS for Kids*, copyright 2004 and 2005; **page 28**, Content courtesy of Serhan Gungor; **page 37**, "The E-Factor!" by Mary C. Hickey, *Ladies' Home Journal*, September 1995. © 1995, Meredith Corporation, all rights reserved. Used with permission of *Ladies' Home Journal*; **page 44**, "Happiness Is . . ." by Andrea Sachs, *TIME*, May 3, 2006. © 2006 Time Inc. Reprinted with permission; **page 53**, "How Color Can Change Your Life" by Pamela Stock, *Mademoiselle*, August 1994. Courtesy of *Mademoiselle*, © 1994 Conde Nast Publications Inc.; **page 57**, "Feng Shui for the Home" by Evelyn Lip, Torrance, California: Heian International, 1996; **page 67**, "The House on Mango Street" by Sandra Cisneros. From *The House on Mango Street* © 1984 by Sandra Cisneros, Vintage Books, division of Random House, Inc., and in hardcover by Alfred A. Knopf, 1994. Reprinted by permission of Susan Bergholz, Literary Services, New York, all rights reserved; **page 72**, "My House" by Daniel Lourie, reprinted by permission; **page 79**, Adapted from "Birth Order: What It Means for Your Kids . . . and You" by Janet Strassman Perlmutter, © June 2004, United Parenting Publications; **page 85**, "The Stones" from *You Can't Have Everything* by Richard Shelton, © 1975. Reprinted by permission of the University of Pittsburgh Press; **page 95**, "Athletes as Role Models" by Sheila Globus, *Current Health*, February 1998. Reprinted with permission, Current Health 2®, © 1998, published by Weekly Reader Corporation, all rights reserved; **page 103**, Adapted from "Olympic Marathons, Then and Now" by Mary Evans Andrews, *Cricket Magazine*, August 2004; **page 113**, "Helping Athletes Go for the Gold" by Robert Epstein, © May/June 1999, *Psychology Today*, © 1991–2006 Sussex Publishers; **page 118**, "It Couldn't Be Done" by Edgar A. Guest, reprinted from *The Collected Verse of Edgar Guest*, © 1934, used by permission of Contemporary Books, Inc, Chicago; **page 127**, "Plant Power" adapted from "Chile Peppers," September 1994 issue of *3-2-1 Contact* Magazine, © 1994 Children's Television Workshop, New York, all rights reserved; **page 134**, Adapted from "Music's Surprising Power to Heal" by David M. Mazie, *Reader's Digest*, August 1992. Reprinted with permission, © 1992 The Reader's Digest Association, Inc.; **page 143**, "Frogs and Human Health" by Bill Sharp, © March/April 1995, Massachusetts Audubon Society, reprinted by permission; **page 159**, "They're Stealing Our Masterpieces" by Ira Chinoy. Condensed from

Providence Sunday Journal Magazine, May 20, 1990, © 1990 by *The Providence Journal-Bulletin*; **page 167**, Adapted from "Crime Lab" by Emily Sohn, reprinted with permission from *SCIENCE NEWS for Kids*, copyright 2004 and 2005; **page 173**, "For Sale: Stolen Animals—The demand for rare pets causes a crisis for endangered species," www.timeforkids.com, © 1998 *TIME for Kids*, reprinted by permission; **page 187**, "Valuable By-Products of Space Research" by David Dooling and Mitchell R. Sharpe, reprinted from *Compton's Interactive Encyclopedia*, © 1992, 1994, 1995 by Compton New Media, Inc. © 1922–1995 Compton's Learning Company, all rights reserved; **page 195**, "Destination Mars" by Emily Sohn, reprinted with permission from *SCIENCE NEWS for Kids*, copyright 2004 and 2005; **page 202**, "Dancing to the Music of Physics," interview reprinted with permission of Dr. Steve Huber; **page 215**, "Nothing but the Truth" by Sean McCollum, *Scholastic Update*, May 7, 1993, © 1993 by Scholastic Inc, reprinted by permission; **page 224**, "Do's and Taboos: Cultural Aspects of International Business" by M. Katherine Glover, *Business America*, August 13, 1990, pp. 2–6, reprinted with permission.

Acknowledgments

We have many people to thank for their valuable input to this second edition of *For Your Information 4*. In particular, we thank Margot Downey, A. K. Kemp, Laura Martin, Robby Steinberg, and Serhan Gungor for their time, the clarity of their critiques, and their good advice. As always, we are indebted to our families, friends, colleagues, and students for their inspiration, kindness, generosity, and support. Many thanks also to Karen Davy for her meticulous attention to the details and to Laura Le Dréan, Gina DiLillo, and Wendy Campbell at Pearson Longman.

We hope that you and your students enjoy the readings and activities in this text and find them interesting *for your information*.

KLB, CBR

Karen Blanchard and Christine Root first met when they were teaching at the University of Pennsylvania. It wasn't long before they began working on their first book, *Ready to Write*. They have continued their successful collaboration, producing more than 17 popular reading and writing textbooks.

Karen has an M.S.Ed. in English Education from the University of Pennsylvania, and Christine has an M.Ed. in English Education from the University of Massachusetts, Boston. Both authors have over 25 years' experience working with English-language learners at the university level. Karen has also taught at the American Language Academy at Beaver College, in addition to tutoring students at many levels. Christine has taught in the Harvard ESL program and is a founder, coordinator, and guide in the ESOL tour program at the Museum of Fine Arts, Boston. Karen and Christine continue to enjoy working together to create English-language textbooks for students around the world.

WHAT LANGUAGES DO YOU SPEAK?

Throughout the world, wherever there is human society, there is language. It is only because we can communicate with one another that we have been able to develop civilizations. Advances in science, technology, economics, the arts, and government are all the results of people communicating.

Points to Ponder

Think about these questions and discuss them in a small group.

1. How many languages do you know? What other languages do you wish you could speak? Why?
2. How do you think a child learns his or her native language? In what ways do you think learning a second language is similar to or different from learning a first language?
3. What are some of the similarities and differences between your native language and English? For example, are the sentence structure and word order similar or different?
4. Do you like the idea of a universal language that everyone in the world could speak? Why or why not?

1

Reaping the Rewards of Learning English

Before You Read

A Learning a new language can be difficult. Which of the following are the most difficult for you in learning English? Check (✔) three items and then compare answers with a partner.

	Your Answers	**Your Partner's Answers**
1. pronunciation		
2. speaking		
3. grammar		
4. vocabulary		
5. listening		
6. idioms and slang		
7. reading		
8. writing		

SKILL FOR SUCCESS ✔

Reading with a Purpose

When you read, it is a good idea to have a **purpose** in mind. This will help you read with a specific goal and keep you actively involved in the reading process. One way to set a purpose is to think of some questions that you would like to have answered in the reading. Then, as you read, look for answers to the questions.

B You are going to read an article about a young girl who moved to the United States from Korea when she was 15 years old. When she arrived, she knew almost no English. But within a few years, she had graduated from high school with honors and written a book. Write three questions you hope will be answered in the article.

1. _____

2. _____

3. _____

C Learn the meanings of the following words before you read the article. The numbers in parentheses indicate the paragraph where the word first appears in the article.

feat (1)   risky (4)   bewildered (6)

qualms (3)   worthwhile (4)   daring (7)

humiliated (3)   evolved (5)   rough (8)

REAPING THE REWARDS OF LEARNING ENGLISH

by Jean Caldwell

1 At Sunday's graduation, Su-Kyeong Kim will speak to the 385 members of her class at Northfield Mount Hermon School. This is an amazing feat for a girl who hardly spoke a word of English when she came here from Korea four years ago at age 15.

2 But Kim herself is amazing. Besides becoming fluent in English, Kim has won numerous academic awards. She has also written a book about her experiences struggling with the English language. The name of her book is *Looking for Trouble*. Her teachers hope she will find a publisher soon for her book.

3 Kim realized the need for the book when she began helping newly arrived Korean students at her school. She realized the newcomers suffered the same qualms she had. "You think you are the only person being embarrassed, humiliated, making mistakes," she said in a recent interview on campus. "But everyone does it."

Su-Kyeong Kim

OK to Make Mistakes

4 Su-Kyeong calls her book *Looking for Trouble* to show that the road to success in mastering a second language is a risky path. "I want others to know that it's OK to make mistakes," she said, "that nothing worthwhile is without risk." Su-Kyeong says, "Lots of

people think other people do not make a lot of mistakes or are not as embarrassed as they are. It's not true. Everyone is embarrassed when they make a mistake, and everyone makes mistakes. You can turn that mistake into a greater step to your success."

5 The book evolved out of a series of papers she wrote for her junior English class. The papers described her experiences as a newcomer to the United States. She wrote about what she called her "hellish arrival" here when she and her mother went frantically back and forth between the airports in New York City because of bad advice. She described their fear on a midnight taxi ride from Boston to Northfield when they could not understand the explanation of their driver when he stopped in a dimly lit parking lot near a dark building.

Innocent Misunderstandings

6 In the book, Su-Kyeong describes misunderstandings that happened because of her limited English. For example, she wrote of her encounter with a teacher who was aghast when she mispronounced the word *sheet* when she asked for a piece of paper. She also explained her bewildered dismay when a student who had asked to sit at her lunch table turned away. The other student had asked, "Do you mind if I sit with you?" Su-Kyeong said, "Yes!" because she had heard, "May I sit with you?"

7 Her advice to people studying a second language: "Look for trouble. Be gutsy. Be daring. You have to dare to learn another language. You can't sit in your own room and

analyze grammar. You have to go and talk to people and listen to them." Su-Kyeong also writes about things that are hard for foreigners. She believes, "One of the hardest things for a foreigner is the feeling of being constantly left out—not deliberately, but by the inadequacy of one's own knowledge of language and culture. Because we want to feel part of the group, we are always watching others' faces to see how the wind blows."

8 Su-Kyeong understands very well how hard it is to learn a new language, and she worked very hard to master English. She explains to her readers, "I started excluding reading when people asked me about my hobbies. No more lying on the bed with my feet on the wall. You can't use ten highlighters and a thick dictionary while you are flat on your back. Instead, I sat up straight and rigid in a hard chair, trying to burn as much new vocabulary and as many fresh idioms into my brain as possible. Sometimes I had to use my dictionary 30 times just to get a rough picture of what was going on."

9 All Su-Kyeong Kim's hard work has paid off. In addition to writing a book and being chosen class speaker at graduation, she also won the English as a Second Language Award in the spring of her freshman year, the Junior Class English Prize, and the Departmental Award for Chinese 2. She also is a member of the Cum Laude Society, which honors superior scholastic achievement. In September, Su-Kyeong will enter Stanford University in California, where she plans to study Japanese and international business.

After You Read

A Read these statements. If a statement is true according to the article, write *T* on the line. If it is false, write *F*.

_____T_____ 1. Kim won many academic awards in high school, including the English as a Second Language Award.

_____T~~F~~_____ 2. Kim was chosen to speak at her high school graduation.

_____F_____ 3. In her book, *Looking for Trouble*, Kim gives advice about how to learn Korean.

_____T_____ 4. *Looking for Trouble* developed from a series of papers Kim wrote for her English class in high school.

_____F_____ 5. When Kim moved to the United States, she was already fluent in English.

_____F_____ 6. Kim and her mother had a wonderful experience when they first arrived in the United States.

_____T_____ 7. Kim believes that foreigners feel left out because they lack knowledge of the language and culture.

_____F_____ 8. Kim studied Chinese as well as English in high school.

_____T_____ 9. Kim intends to study Japanese and international business at Stanford University.

SKILL FOR SUCCESS

Summarizing

Summarizing is a good way to help you understand an article and remember what you read. When you summarize, you should write about the important ideas in the reading using your own words.

B Using your own words, complete the summary.

Su-Kyeong Kim is an amazing girl. She came _to the United States_
1.
when _she was 15_____, knowing almost _____.
2.   3.
Since then, she has accomplished many feats. For example, she has
_____, won _numerous academic awards_, and was
4.   5.
chosen _speak at graduation_. Kim also _written a book_
6.   7.
called _Looking for Trouble_. In the book, Kim writes about
8.
_hellish arrival_____ and gives advice to _people_____.
9.   10.

She wants other people to know that it is _____.
                                                                    11.

In the fall, Kim will _____.
                                        12.

A **Choose the word or phrase that is closest in meaning to the underlined word in each sentence.**

1. This is an amazing <u>feat</u> for a girl who hardly spoke a word of English when she came here from Korea four years ago at age 15.
   a. language
   b. accomplishment
   c. mistake

English is the native language in 34 countries and a significant language in 104 countries. Approximately 14 percent of the world's population speaks English.

2. Kim realized the need for the book when she began helping newly arrived Korean students at her school. She realized the newcomers suffered the same <u>qualms</u> she had.
   a. success
   b. doubts
   c. needs

3. Su-Kyeong calls her book *Looking for Trouble* to show that the road to success in mastering a second language is a <u>risky</u> path.
   a. dangerous
   b. easy
   c. long

4. The book <u>evolved</u> out of a series of papers she wrote for her junior English class.
   a. copied
   b. described
   c. developed

5. Sometimes I had to use my dictionary 30 times just to get a <u>rough</u> picture of what was going on.
   a. certain
   b. approximate
   c. violent

6. You think you are the only person being embarrassed, <u>humiliated</u>, or making mistakes.
   a. shamed
   b. admired
   c. confused

Over 700 million people speak English as a foreign language.

7. "I want others to know . . . ," she said, "that nothing <u>worthwhile</u> is without risk.
   a. sensitive
   b. worthless
   c. valuable   #worth less

8. She also explained her <u>bewildered</u> dismay when a student who had asked to sit at her lunch table turned away.
   a. confused
   b. amused
   c. critical

9. Look for trouble. Be gutsy. Be <u>daring</u>. You have to dare to learn another language.
   a. shy and keeping quiet
   b. brave and taking risks
   c. loud and making noise

B Cross out the word in each group that does not belong.

1. risky   hazardous   ~~exhausting~~   dangerous

2. specific   vague   rough   approximate

3. bewildered   wild   confused   perplexed

4. daring   gutsy   hesitant   brave

5. humiliated   delighted   embarrassed   ashamed

6. feat   defeat   achievement   accomplishment

7. valuable   unusual   useful   worthwhile

8. apprehension   qualm   doubt   humor

9. developed   evolved   received   grew

 SKILL FOR SUCCESS

Learning Synonyms
Synonyms are words that have similar meanings. For example, *precise* and *exact* are synonyms because they mean almost the same thing. Learning synonyms can help you improve your vocabulary.

C Complete the chart. Find a synonym for each word from the article. Use the list below.

accomplishment   dangerous   fear

adventurous   developed   general

confused   embarrassed   valuable

Word	Synonym
1. risky	*dangerous*
2. rough	
3. daring	
4. humiliated	
5. worthwhile	
6. qualm	
7. evolved	
8. feat	
9. bewildered	

D Complete the e-mail with words from the Synonym column in Exercise C. Be sure to use the correct form of the words.

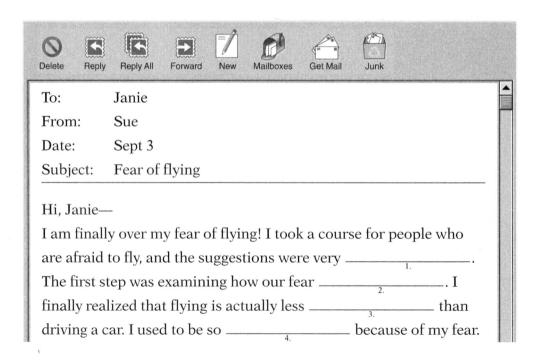

To: Janie

From: Sue

Date: Sept 3

Subject: Fear of flying

Hi, Janie—

I am finally over my fear of flying! I took a course for people who are afraid to fly, and the suggestions were very _____. 1.

The first step was examining how our fear _____. 2. I finally realized that flying is actually less _____ 3. than driving a car. I used to be so _____ 4. because of my fear.

I thought my friends laughed at me behind my back. But now I think I can fly anywhere. For my first flight, I went to Atlanta to visit my brother. It was a two-hour flight. When we landed, I knew it was a real _____ for me. My _____ about flying were finally over! Maybe someday I'll be _____ enough to go parachuting! Just kidding. But maybe I'll fly to Boston to visit you!

5.
6.
7.

Talk It Over

Discuss these questions as a class.

1. Do you agree with Kim's advice about learning a new language? Why or why not?
2. If you were writing a book like Kim's, what advice would you give to others learning a second language? What would the title of your book be?
3. Would you be interested in reading Kim's book? Why or why not?
4. How would you describe Kim? What kind of person do you think she is?

✓ **Summarizing**

Reading about Scientific Research

Read the following short article, which describes research into the different ways that children and adults learn a second language. Then answer the questions that follow the article. Finally, use your answers to write a one-paragraph summary of the article.

The Bilingual Brain

When Karl Kim immigrated to the United States from Korea as a teenager ten years ago, he had some difficulty learning English. Now he speaks it fluently, and recently he had a unique opportunity to see how our brains adapt to a second language. Kim is a graduate student in the lab of Joy Hirsch, a neuroscientist at Memorial Sloan-Kettering Cancer Center in New York. He and Hirsch recently found evidence that children and adults do not use the same parts of the brain when learning a second language.

The researchers used an instrument called a functional magnetic resonance imager (fMRI) to study the brains of two groups of bilingual people. One group consisted of people who had learned a second language as children. The other consisted of those who, like Kim, learned their second language later in life. The fMRI scanner allows Kim and Hirsch to see which parts of a person's brain are active when the person thinks. Kim and Hirsch asked people from both groups to think about what they had done the day before, first in one language and then in the other, and scanned their brains.

Kim and Hirsch looked specifically at two language centers in the brain. One is called *Wernicke's area*, in the rear of the brain, which is believed to process the meaning of language. The other is called *Broca's area*, in the left frontal part, which is thought to manage speech production. Both groups of people, Kim and Hirsch found, used the same part of Wernicke's area no matter what language they were speaking. But their use of Broca's area was different for their second language.

How does Hirsch account for this difference? There are several possibilities. One is that when language is being hard-wired in children, the brain may combine sounds and structures from all languages into the same area. But after that wiring is complete, the management of a new language, with new sounds and new structures, must be taken over by a different part of the brain.

A second possibility is simply that we may acquire languages differently as children than we do as adults. "If you watch mothers or family members teaching an infant to speak," says Hirsch, "it's very tactile[1], it's very auditory[2], it's very visual. There are a lot of different inputs. And that's very different from sitting in a classroom."

[1] **tactile** – related to the sense of touch

[2] **auditory** – related to hearing

1. *Who* did the research? _____

2. *Where* was the research conducted? _____

3. *Who* and *what* did they study? _____
   _____

4. *What* parts of the brain did they study? _____

5. *What* did they discover? _____
   _____

6. What are the two reasons given for the difference in how children and adults learn a second language?
   a. _____
   _____
   b. _____
   _____

UNIT 1

CHAPTER 2

The Hope of Esperanto

Before You Read

SKILL FOR SUCCESS ✓

Previewing and Predicting
Before they read, good readers **preview** the text and **predict**, or guess, what it will be about. Here's how to do it. First, preview the text by looking it over. Read the title and subtitle, section headings, and words in bold print or italics. Also look at the pictures and read the captions. All of these will help you predict the content of the reading. Previewing and predicting will help you understand what you read more easily.

A Preview the article by looking at the title, subtitle, headings, words in italics, and photos. Also read the caption under the second photo. Then make predictions by checking (✓) the topics you think will be discussed.

❏ 1. The history of Esperanto
❏ 2. Information about Ludovic Zamenhof
❏ 3. The English grammar system
❏ 4. Esperanto in the arts
❏ 5. The use of Esperanto on the Internet
❏ 6. Learning Esperanto
❏ 7. How to invent your own language

B Learn the meanings of the following words and phrases before you read the article.

artificial (1)   embraced (3)   exceptions (5)
vision (2)   participants (4)   advocates (5)
ups and downs (3)

The Hope of Esperanto

A Language without Borders

1 Although our world is growing smaller through the Internet, the global economy, and improved transportation, people still have difficulty communicating with one another. Thousands of languages are spoken around the world today. Some people think that the answer to the problems in global communication is the use of an artificial international language that allows people who speak different native languages to communicate with one another. One such language is Esperanto.

2 Esperanto was the vision of Ludovic Zamenhof, a Polish doctor who wanted to construct a simple language that could be learned and spoken by people all over the world. He worked for many years to make his dream a reality, and in 1887 he published a small booklet, *Lingvo Internacia (International Language)*, under the pseudonym Dr. Esperanto, which means "one who hopes." His pseudonym was soon adopted as the name of his language. He did not intend for Esperanto to replace any of the world's languages but for it to serve as an additional second language.

The Ups and Downs of Esperanto

3 Esperanto has had an interesting history. In 1904, the first group of Esperanto speakers met in France. They tested the oral use of the language and found that Esperanto was a good way to communicate. In the years that followed, Esperanto began to spread around Europe. Over the years, Esperanto has had its ups and downs. According to journalist J. D. Reed, "The use of Esperanto probably reached its peak in the 1920s, when idealists embraced it as one small step toward peace. Some intellectuals viewed it as a solution to the language problem, which they felt contributed to political misunderstandings. In some British schools, in fact, youngsters could study Esperanto. But interest died down after World War II, partly because governments did not support the language, and partly because English was fast becoming the language of business and travel. Esperantists have urged the United Nations to adopt their language, but the U.N. has its hands full[1] with six official languages

Ludovic Zamenhof invented an international language that could be spoken by people all over the world.

---

[1] **have one's hands full** – to have a lot to do

(English, French, Spanish, Arabic, Chinese, and Russian)."

4 For a while, people worried that Esperanto would die out; however, it has survived, and today Esperanto is spoken all over the world. Esperanto speakers can be found in 90 countries in Europe, Asia, Australia, and North and South America. It is estimated that between 1 and 2 million people worldwide speak Esperanto. And Esperanto is taught as a second language in schools in China, Hungary, and Bulgaria. International meetings of Esperanto speakers are held every year. Over 2,300 participants from 62 countries attended the 90th World Esperanto Congress in Vilnius, Lithuania, in July 2005.

Mastering Esperanto

5 Many people who study Esperanto say that it is easy to learn. The grammar is logical, with only 16 simple rules and no exceptions. The word forms are easy to learn, too. All nouns in Esperanto end in *o*, adjectives end in *a*, and infinitive verbs end in *i*. Advocates of Esperanto claim that anyone can learn Esperanto in only 100 hours or less. But others think Esperanto's numerous suffixes and prefixes make it more difficult.

Movies, Music, Museums, and More

6 Esperanto is used for academic and artistic works, too. Over 100 magazines and journals are published in Esperanto.

And there is no lack of Esperanto literature, with more than 25,000 books in circulation. Novels, poems, and short stories have all been written in Esperanto. In 1999 and 2000, the Scottish author William Auld was nominated for the Nobel Prize for literature for his writings in Esperanto. In addition, thousands of books written in other languages have been translated into Esperanto. There are several movies produced entirely in Esperanto as well. Jacques-Louis Mahé produced the first full-length feature film in Esperanto, entitled *Angoroj*, in 1964. This was followed in 1965 by *Incubus*, starring William Shatner. Radio broadcasts in Esperanto can be heard on stations such as Radio Beijing in China. There is even an international Esperanto museum in Vienna, Austria.

Esperanto on the Internet

7 Thanks to the Internet, Esperanto is spreading like never before. You can click on Web sites dedicated to teaching Esperanto online and participate in chat rooms to practice communicating using Esperanto. There are even Web sites where you can download music in Esperanto. Esperanto is alive and well. Recently, Esperanto has spread to countries such as Mongolia and Indonesia. In Hungary, Esperanto is the third most widely spoken foreign language. There is no doubt that Esperanto has found a place for itself in today's world. ■

After You Read

Comprehension Check

A Read these statements. If a statement is true according to the article, write *T* on the line. If it is false, write *F*.

_____ 1. The goal of Esperanto is to help people who speak the same language communicate with one another.

_____ 2. Esperanto is a dying language.

_____ 3. The total number of Esperantists is 8 million.

_____ 4. Everyone agrees that Esperanto is a simple language to learn.

_____ 5. The use of Esperanto has decreased since the 1920s.

_____ 6. Esperanto is used to make communication easier among people who do not speak the same language.

_____ 7. Many literary works can be read in Esperanto.

_____ 8. Esperanto is Hungary's most widely spoken language.

_____ 9. In recent years, the Internet has helped to spread Esperanto.

_____ 10. Esperanto is spoken on the radio in China.

_____ 11. Poetry, music, and even movies are written in Esperanto.

_____ 12. Esperanto will soon be the most popular language in the world.

✓ **Summarizing**

B Using your own words, write a one-paragraph summary of the article. Use these questions to help you.

1. Who invented Esperanto? Why? When?
2. What are the benefits of Esperanto?
3. What is Esperanto used for?

_____

_____

_____

_____

_____

_____

Vocabulary Practice

A Match each word or phrase with the correct definition.

	Word or Phrase		Definition
_e_	**1.** artificial	**a.**	someone who takes part in something
___	**2.** embrace	**b.**	good times and bad times
___	**3.** ups and downs	**c.**	a dream
___	**4.** participant	**d.**	to eagerly accept ideas and opinions
___	**5.** advocate	**e.**	made by human beings, not natural
___	**6.** exception	**f.**	something that does not fit into the general rules
___	**7.** vision	**g.**	someone who supports something

B Complete each sentence with the correct word or phrase from Exercise A. Be sure to use the correct form of the words.

1. The economy has had _____ over the past few years.

2. Ludovic Zamenhof's _____ was to create an _____ language that could be learned and spoken by people all over the world.

3. _____ of Esperanto hope that the number of speakers will increase.

4. There are many _____ to the rules of English grammar.

5. Most of the _____ in the conference stayed at the same hotel.

6. Not everyone _____ the idea of a universal language.

SKILL FOR SUCCESS

Understanding Word Parts: The Suffixes *-ant* and *-ent*
A **suffix** is a letter or group of letters that is added to the end of a word. Suffixes change the meaning or part of speech of the word.
   Some verbs can be changed into nouns by adding the suffix *-ant* or *-ent*. These suffixes mean "a person or thing performing or causing an action." In this chapter, you learned the word *participant*. It is formed by adding the suffix *-ant* to the verb *participate*.

C Complete the chart by writing the correct definition from the list below next to each word.

Word	Definition
1. resident	*A person who resides, or has his or her home, in a place*
2. accountant	
3. servant	
4. dependent	
5. opponent	
6. defendant	
7. assistant	

Definitions

Someone who opposes a particular idea or action

A person who is accused of a crime and needs to be defended

A person who examines the financial records of a company

Someone who assists someone else to do a job

Someone who depends on you for financial support

~~A person who resides, or has his or her home, in a place~~

A person who serves someone by doing jobs in his or her home

D Complete each sentence with the correct word from the chart in Exercise C. Be sure to use the correct form of the words.

1. Our office _____ helps me by answering the phone, scheduling appointments, and entering information into the computer.

2. My two young children are my _____.

3. The _____ in this trial is accused of committing robbery.

4. None of the _____ of this building are allowed to have pets.

5. Please have your _____ check the financial records from last year.

6. In the past, rich people often had _____ in their homes to do the housework and chores.

7. The _____ of the mayor's bill voted against it.

Discuss these questions as a class.

1. Would you be interested in learning an artificial language such as Esperanto?
2. Do you think the idea of an invented universal language is a good one? What would it be useful for? What problems might it solve? What problems might it cause?
3. Can you translate this passage from Esperanto into English? (The answer is upside down at the bottom of this page.)

> Je unua rigardo, Esperanto ŝajnas sufiĉe simpla.
> La lingvo havas nur 16 facile memoreblajn
> gramatikajn regulojn—sen iuj ajn esceptoj—kaj
> bazan vortaron konstruitan el plejparte hindeŭropaj
> radikoj.

Reading an Autobiography

An autobiography is a book about a person's life, written by that person. The following excerpt is from *Lost in Translation: A Life in a New Language*, the autobiography of Eva Hoffman. Ms. Hoffman was born in Krakow, Poland, and immigrated to Vancouver, Canada, when she was 13.

Study the vocabulary words below, read the passage on page 18, and then answer the questions that follow the passage.

demonstrative—willing to show your feelings
gesticulations—movements with your hands when you talk
reserve—the quality of being unwilling to show your feelings
restraint—calm and controlled behavior
intimacy—the state of having a close personal relationship with someone

> At a glance, Esperanto seems simple enough. It has only 16 easily memorized rules of grammar—no exceptions—and a basic vocabulary built from mostly Indo-European roots.

Lost in Translation: A Life in a New Language

by Eva Hoffman

My mother says I'm becoming English. This hurts me, because I know she means I'm becoming cold. I'm no colder than I've ever been, but I'm learning to be less demonstrative. I learn this from a teacher who, after contemplating the gesticulations with which I help myself describe the digestive system of a frog, tells me to "sit on my hands and then try talking." I learn my new reserve from people who take a step back when we talk, because I'm standing too close, crowding them. Cultural distances are different, I later learn in a sociology class, but I know it already. I learn restraint from Penny, who looks offended when I shake her by the arm in excitement, as if my gesture had been one of aggression instead of friendliness. I learn it from a girl who pulls away when I hook my arm through hers as we walk down the street—this movement of friendly intimacy is an embarrassment to her.

I learn also that certain kinds of truth are impolite. One shouldn't criticize the person one is with, at least not directly. You shouldn't say, "You are wrong about that," although you may say, "On the other hand, there is that to consider." You shouldn't say, "This doesn't look good on you," although you may say, "I like you better in that other outfit." I learn to tone down[1] my sharpness . . .

Perhaps my mother is right, after all; perhaps I'm becoming colder. After a while, emotion follows action, response grows warmer or cooler according to gesture. I'm more careful about what I say, how loud I laugh, whether I give vent to[2] grief. ■

[1] **tone down** – to make something less intense or offensive

[2] **give vent to** – to express a strong feeling

1. Why do you think the author named her autobiography *Lost in Translation*? Do you think it is an appropriate title? Why?
2. In what ways is the author becoming less demonstrative?
3. How is she learning her new reserve?
4. What did she learn about *truth*?
5. According to the author, what is the relationship between emotion and gesture?

UNIT 1

CHAPTER 3

Instant Messaging: Shaping Our Lives

A Think about these questions and discuss them in a small group.

1. Do you use e-mail to communicate with your friends and family? How often?
2. Would you rather meet with old friends online or in person? What about new friends? Do you think you would feel more comfortable communicating with someone you don't know online or face to face?
3. What do you think are the advantages and disadvantages of communicating with e-mail?

SKILL FOR SUCCESS

Using Background Knowledge

Before you read a passage, it is a good idea to think about what you already know about the subject. This is called **using your background knowledge.** You will understand what you read more easily when you connect the new information in the reading with information that you already know.

B Think about what you know about using the Internet to communicate with other people. Check (✔) the statements you agree with. Then compare answers with a partner.

☐ 1. The Internet has changed the way we communicate.
☐ 2. There is only one way to communicate using the Internet.
☐ 3. Many people use e-mail to send messages to others.
☐ 4. Languages never change.
☐ 5. Scientists study the way we communicate.
☐ 6. Some languages around the world are dying out.
☐ 7. There is a difference between the way men and women communicate on the Internet.

Skimming for the Main Idea
Skimming is a way of reading quickly to get the *gist*, or main idea, of the content of a reading. It is a useful technique because it gives you an overview of the passage and an idea about how it is organized.

   When you skim, you don't read every word carefully or stop to look up words you don't know in a dictionary. To skim an article, read the first and last paragraphs. (The first paragraph often introduces the main idea of the passage, and the last paragraph may sum it up.) Then skim the whole passage by reading the first and last sentence of every paragraph. Notice any headings, pictures, charts, and graphs. Also pay attention to words in italics, lists, and pull-out quotes that often identify important information.

C Skim the article one time. Circle the correct answer.

   1. What is the article about?
      a. how the Internet has changed the way we communicate
      b. changes in the field of linguistics

   2. The article discusses _____.
      a. only the negative effects of the Internet on communication
      b. the positive and negative effects of the Internet on communication

D Learn the meanings of the following words before you read the article.

multiple (5)	alarming (11)	abandoning (11)
sloppy (7)	neglecting (11)	revitalize (11)
submitted (7)		

Instant Messaging: Shaping Our Lives

by Emily Sohn

1   The Internet has revolutionized the way we communicate. Every day, billions of e-mail messages are sent and received. People e-mail friends next door and relatives on the other side of the world. Instead of waiting a few days for a letter to arrive at its destination, you can send an e-mail that will get there in minutes or even seconds. But for some people, even e-mail is too slow. Today, more and more people—especially teenagers and college students—use an even faster method of communication: instant messaging (IMing).

4 = for	**g/g (or g2g)** = got to go
bc (or b/c) = because	**k** = OK
bf = boyfriend	**lol** = laughing out loud
gf = girlfriend	(or lots of love)
btw = by the way	**ttyl** = talk to you later
CU = see you	**y?** = why?

2   The following is part of a conversation between two college students, Gale and Sally.

Gale: hey g2g
Sally: k
Sally: I'll ttyl?
Gale: gotta do errands
Gale: yep!!!
Sally: k
Sally: :-)
Gale: ttyl
Sally: alrighty

3   It would sound silly to say these words out loud. But the conversation made sense when Gale and Sally were IMing them to each other on their computers. Each person could see what the other was writing every time one of them pressed the return key, even though they were in different places.

A New Branch of Study

4   Linguists are studying instant messaging, cell phone text messages, and e-mails to try to understand how technology is changing the way we communicate. One group of researchers is fascinated by the interaction between language and the Internet. "The Internet is allowing us to explore language in a creative way," says David Crystal, a linguist at the University of Wales. "This is a new branch of study. Like no other study of language change in history, the Internet allows us to follow the rate of change of grammar, pronunciation, and vocabulary."

Computer Talk

5   Researchers have a name for instant messages, cell phone text messages, and e-mail. They call it computer-mediated communication, or CMC. CMC is different from speech in a number of ways, Crystal says. For one thing, you can have multiple IM conversations at once, which you can't have when you're talking directly to people. However, with CMC, you lose the effect of emotion and tone of voice, no matter how many "smiley faces[1]" you use.

Patterns in Instant Messaging

6   Studying IM conversations can also be an interesting way to learn more about culture, relationships, and differences between men and women, says Naomi

[1] smiley face – ☺

Baron, a linguist at American University in Washington, D.C. In one study, Baron analyzed 23 IM conversations between college students (including the one at the beginning of this article). In total, there were 2,185 transmissions and 11,718 words. She was surprised by what her data showed.

7 For one thing, the messages were far less sloppy than she expected. Students seemed to be careful about what they wrote, and they usually corrected their mistakes. In fact, she says, students seemed to pay more attention to what they said in messages than they did in papers submitted for grading.

8 There were also major differences between men's and women's use of IM technology. Men tended to write in short phrases, while women tended to write in complete sentences. Women also took longer to say good-bye to each other. Baron concluded that messaging between women is more like writing than speech but messaging between men is more like speech than writing.

9 From questionnaires, Baron learned that most young people have between one and twelve IM conversations going on at once. "I couldn't imagine just having one IM conversation," one student said. "That would just be too weird." Before the invention of CMC, having that many conversations at once would have been practically impossible. These patterns suggest that IMing is something completely new in the history of communication, Baron says.

Increased Internet Activity

10 In recent years, the rise in the use of Internet communication has been greatest among young people. The United States accounts for 20 percent of all Internet activity, says Brenda Danet, a researcher at Yale University in Connecticut and Hebrew University in Jerusalem. Still, more and more people of all ages are using the Internet for longer amounts of time in countries around the world, especially in places such as China. And nonnative English speakers make up at least two-thirds of Internet users, Danet says.

11 Nonetheless, her research has shown that English is used most of the time on international mailing lists because it's the language that most people have at least some knowledge of. Languages have been dying out at an alarming rate, and the wide use of English online makes many linguists worry that people are neglecting their own languages and abandoning their own cultures. It's also true, however, that the Internet has opened up many possibilities for rapid communication across cultures. And the Internet might also be a good forum for the preservation of disappearing languages. "Is the Internet contributing to the extinction of languages, or can it help revitalize them?" Danet asks. Only time will tell.

Shaping Our Lives

12 In the meantime, CMC seems to be here to stay, says communications researcher Simeon Yates of Sheffield Hallam University. The more we use IM, text messaging on our cell phones, and other new technologies, he says, the more they shape our lives and relationships. People can now manage their schedules

from anywhere and change plans at the last minute. They can send text messages to each other over their phones without making a sound. People have even discovered ways to express complicated feelings and emotions in only a few words. A few generations ago, no one could have imagined that we would be communicating over computers in real time without ever speaking a word, Yates says. Now, people feel helpless without their e-mail and cell phones. "When I ask British college students what they would do if I took their cell phones away," says Yates, "they say they couldn't live without them."

13   New technologies may open up additional communication possibilities in the future. So, keep typing away. Just remember that technology shapes you every time you use it. And that could be a good thing or a bad thing, depending on how you look at it.

14   *yup. OK 4 now. CU soon. ttyl!!!*

After You Read

Comprehension Check

A Read these statements. If a statement is true according to the article, write *T* on the line. If it is false, write *F*.

_____ 1. The Internet has caused a big change in the way we communicate.

_____ 2. It isn't normal for a language to change over time.

_____ 3. Linguists have different opinions about the future of languages.

_____ 4. Men and women use IM technology differently.

_____ 5. The greatest rise in Internet communication has been among older people.

B Circle the correct answer.

1. According to the article, some language experts are worried that computers are _____.
   a. too expensive for everyone to use
   b. forcing people to neglect their native languages
   c. helping people learn the rules of grammar

2. Which is NOT an example of computer-mediated communication?
   a. an e-mail message
   b. an instant message
   c. a handwritten letter

3. The author points out that CMC is _____.
   a. different from speech and normal writing
   b. similar to both speech and normal writing
   c. more similar to speech than to normal writing

4. Naomi Baron was surprised that students she studied _____.
   a. wrote sloppy IM messages
   b. were careful about what they wrote
   c. wrote 2,185 transmissions

5. Which is true about the differences between men and women in how they used IM technology?
   a. Messaging between men is more like speech.
   b. Messaging between women is more like speech.
   c. Men usually write longer phrases.

6. According to Brenda Danet, _____.
   a. most Internet users are native speakers of English
   b. nonnative English speakers rarely use the Internet
   c. most Internet users are nonnative speakers of English

7. Simeon Yates believes that computer-mediated communication _____.
   a. is just a passing fad
   b. will not change in the future
   c. is here to stay

SKILL
FOR
SUCCESS

Identifying Facts and Opinions
Facts are statements that can be proven to be true. Opinions are statements that describe someone's feelings or beliefs about a topic. The ability to distinguish between facts and opinions will help you to make judgments about what you read. It is not always easy to recognize the difference between a fact and an opinion, but opinions often use value adjectives such as:

alarming	effective	interesting
appropriate	enormous	lucky
beautiful	excellent	terrible
brilliant	exciting	unfortunate
creative	fascinating	wonderful

C Decide if each statement is a fact or an opinion. Check (✔) the correct box.

	Fact	Opinion
1. Every day, billions of e-mail messages are sent and received.		
2. Studying IM conversations can also be an interesting way to learn more about culture, relationships, and differences between men and women.		
3. CMC is different from speech in a number of ways.		
4. Languages have been dying out at an alarming rate.		
5. In recent years, the rise in the use of Internet communication has been greatest among young people.		
6. The Internet is allowing us to explore language in a creative way.		
7. Nonnative English speakers make up at least two-thirds of Internet users.		
8. Just remember that technology shapes you every time you use it.		

Vocabulary Practice

A Match each word with the correct definition.

Word	Definition
_____ **1.** revitalize	**a.** causing fear
_____ **2.** alarming	**b.** to give up something or someone that was your responsibility
_____ **3.** neglect	
_____ **4.** abandon	**c.** to give to someone in authority, like a teacher
_____ **5.** multiple	**d.** to give new life or energy to something
_____ **6.** sloppy	**e.** many
_____ **7.** submit	**f.** to fail to give care or attention to something or someone
	g. filled with mistakes; not neat or careful

B Complete each sentence with the correct word from Exercise A. Be sure to use the correct form of the words.

1. After the accident, we had to _____ the car and go look for help.

2. Sue spent so much time socializing that she _____ her schoolwork.

3. The paper you _____ to the teacher was _____ and filled with grammar mistakes.

4. The new businesses that moved here _____ the economy of our city in less than a year.

5. I need you to make _____ copies of this report.

6. The fire is spreading at an _____ rate.

SKILL
FOR
SUCCESS

Learning Word Forms

Many English words have verb, noun, and adjective forms. Some have adverb forms, too. When you learn a new word, it is helpful to learn the other words that are related to it. Knowing the meanings of the different **forms of a word** and how to use them correctly will expand your vocabulary and improve your reading fluency.

C Complete the chart. You may need to use your dictionary for help with spelling.

Verb	Noun	Adjective	Adverb
1. invent	*invention*		inventively
2.		responsive	
3.	creation		
4. educate			
5.			conclusively
6. suggest		suggestive	
7.	interaction		
8.		complicated	
9. communicate			

D Correct the sentences with mistakes.

complicated

1. The rules to this game are very ~~complication~~.

2. It is impossible to prove conclusive that he started the fire on purpose.

3. We need to educate our children about the dangers of doing drugs.

4. He made a very good suggest at the meeting.

5. Please response as soon as you get the e-mail.

6. Do you know who invented the camera?

7. The purpose of the game is for students to interaction in a group.

8. I communicate with most of my friends by e-mail.

9. She is the most creatively person I know.

Read a Narrative

In this chapter, you have read that the Internet has changed the way we communicate. Today you can find just about anything on the Web, but does that include finding a wife?

Read the story on page 28 to find out. Then, in a small group, discuss the questions that follow the story.

A Musical Connection

What do you do when it's late at night and you can't sleep? Do you watch television? Read a book? Or do you go to your computer and enter an Internet chat room?

That's what Serhan Gungor does. By profession, Serhan is a tour guide in his native country, Turkey. But his passion is music. So when he can't sleep, he likes to go to music chat rooms and see what people are talking about. Sometimes the conversation gets really interesting and even life-changing, like the time five years ago when Fatosh Dilek entered the chat room. It was 3:00 A.M., and Fatosh had just flown home to Turkey from California, where she had been studying at the University of California at Berkeley. Jet-lagged and unable to sleep, she, too, wanted to talk about her passion: music. Serhan and Fatosh began talking about their favorite subject, jazz, but before long they realized they were talking about themselves—not music! Serhan was impressed with Fatosh's knowledge of

music, but he was also struck by her beautiful use of language, grammar, and punctuation, things that are important to him. She was intrigued by his knowledge of music, his gift for writing, and his directness. By 4:00 A.M., Serhan knew he had to meet this woman, and he invited her to meet him in an hour for a drink! She said no, but they chatted some more. It seemed they had a lot in common.

Because using the Internet is such a dangerous way to meet people, both Serhan and Fatosh conducted reference checks on each other. Both of them were very pleased with what they learned. After three more days of nearly constant e-mailing, Serhan again invited her out. This time she accepted. When he picked her up at her family's house, it was love at first sight. They married a year later in their home city of Istanbul and had a huge celebration with 450 guests.

Isn't it ironic that sometimes it takes something as powerful as the Internet to help us find someone who lives right down the street?!

1. What is your reaction to Serhan and Fatosh's love story?
2. Do you ever go into Internet chat rooms? If so, what topics do you like to discuss?
3. Have you ever talked to anyone in a chat room whom you would like to meet in person? If so, have you met him or her?
4. Do you know anyone who has found a husband or wife using an online dating service or a chat room on the Internet? How did he or she find out if it was safe to meet the person?
5. What do you do when it's late at night and you can't sleep?

Tie It All Together

Discussion

Discuss these questions in a small group.

1. Do you think the people of your country could accept the idea of a universal language? Why or why not?
2. What do you think each of the following sayings means?
   a. Sticks and stones may break my bones, but words will never hurt me.
   b. The pen is mightier than the sword.
   c. Talk is cheap.
   d. Actions speak louder than words.
3. Do you think it's easier to learn a second language as a child or as an adult? Why?
4. Do you think technology is having a positive or a negative effect on the languages of the world? Why?

Just for Fun

Communicating in cyberspace can be fascinating, but without physical clues such as intonation and body language, it is often difficult to get your message across. For this reason, many people use a set of symbols called *emoticons*. Everything from a wink to sticking out your tongue can be conveyed with a few keystrokes.

Match the e-mail emoticons on the left to their correct meanings on the right. Write the correct letter on the line. Hint: Try turning the page sideways to view some of the symbols as faces.

Emoticons	Meanings
___*b*___ **1.** :)	**a.** mad
_____ **2.** :O	**b.** happy
_____ **3.** >:<	**c.** sad
_____ **4.** : D	**d.** laughing
_____ **5.** :-<	**e.** really happy
_____ **6.** :-/	**f.** surprised
_____ **7.** :-e	**g.** disappointed

———— **8.** :(	**h.** hugs
———— **9.** :,(	**i.** kisses
———— **10.** :-o	**j.** crying
———— **11.** :->	**k.** screaming
———— **12.** :	**l.** skeptical
———— **13.** :*	**m.** really sad
———— **14.** []	**n.** tired

abcNEWS

The IM Code

When you write an e-mail, are you careful to use correct punctuation and spelling, or do you focus instead on getting your ideas across quickly? Are your rules for writing e-mail, text messages, and instant messages different from the rules you follow when you write a letter or an essay?

A Study these words. Then watch the video.

acronyms	consuming	frets
alien	conventions	lingo
bonding	etiquette	violating

B Read these questions and then watch the video again. Write an answer to each question.

1. According to the video, who is more likely to use abbreviations in instant messages and other electronic communication—teenagers or adults? Give an example from the video.

   _____

   _____

2. What explanation does Professor Naomi Baron give for the rising popularity of abbreviated language among texting teens?

   _____

   _____

3. What does author Lynne Truss think about the informal language of e-mail and instant messaging? Support your answer with an example from the video.

   _____

   _____

4. Do teenagers agree with Truss? According to the video, what is their view of the code they use to communicate?

_____

_____

C Discuss these questions with a partner or in a small group.

1. If you receive a message using symbols and abbreviated words, can you read that "language" easily, or do you find it difficult to understand?

2. What is your opinion of the e-mail and IM code? Do abbreviations ruin a language, or do they make communication more efficient? Is this code becoming a separate language, or is it just a sloppy form of more conventional language?

Reader's Journal

After you finish each unit in this book, you will write for ten to twenty minutes in the space provided on pages 251–254. This is called a Reader's Journal. The purpose of the task is to help you reflect, in writing, on the ideas and information in each unit. Another purpose is to help you gain fluency without worrying about spelling, grammar, or punctuation. Just try to write as much as you can in English.

Think about the topics and ideas you have read about and discussed in this unit. Pick a topic from the following list, choose one of the discussion questions in the unit, or write about an idea of your own. Write about it for ten to twenty minutes.

- your experience learning a new language
- language and the Internet
- the use of an artificial language like Esperanto

Complete each sentence with the correct word or phrase.

A artificial   neglect   submit
    evolved   revitalize   vision
    humiliated   sloppy

1. I think the Internet will help _____ dying languages.

2. Esperanto is an example of a(n) _____ language.

3. Scientists do not know for sure how languages _____ and developed over time.

4. Ludovic Zamenhof had a(n) _____ of a language that could be learned and spoken by people all over the world.

5. You shouldn't _____ a paper that is _____ and filled with mistakes.

6. Parents should take care of their children, not _____ them.

7. I was _____ when I forgot to bring a birthday gift to the party.

B abandon   exception   ups and downs
    alarming   multiple   worthwhile
    embrace   qualms

1. The huge number of animals that are becoming extinct is _____.

2. I hope you don't _____ your own family values when you get married.

3. I can give you _____ reasons not to start smoking.

4. There is a(n) _____ to almost every rule of English grammar.

5. At first I had _____ about going camping, but it turned out to be a(n) _____ experience.

6. I try to _____ the culture of every country I visit.

7. The company has had its _____, but it's doing very well now.

C advocate   feat   rough
   bewildered   participants
   daring   risky

1. It's _____ to drive on icy roads.

2. Do you have a(n) _____ idea how much this car costs?

3. The children were _____ when a new teacher walked into the room.

4. You should be _____ for once and come mountain climbing with me.

5. Painting the whole house in two days was quite a(n) _____ for me.

6. I am a strong _____ of free speech.

7. All the _____ in the contest must be at least 18 years old.

DON'T WORRY, BE HAPPY

Why are some people happy and enthusiastic most of the time while others are more depressed and pessimistic? Scientists are interested in investigating the causes of our feelings and moods. As you read the articles in this unit, think about your own opinions about happiness.

Points to Ponder

Think about these questions and discuss them in a small group.

1. What things put you in a good mood? What things put you in a bad mood?
2. Do you get into a bad mood often? What do you do to get yourself into a better mood?
3. Which of the following can affect your moods? Check (✔) them.

☐ **a.** weather ☐ **e.** sleep
☐ **b.** music ☐ **f.** your job or school
☐ **c.** food ☐ **g.** colors
☐ **d.** physical exercise ☐ **h.** other:

The E-Factor!

Before You Read

A Discuss these questions with a partner.

1. Generally speaking, are you an optimist or a pessimist?
2. The article you are about to read is called "The E-Factor!" The "E" stands for *enthusiasm*. How would you define the word *enthusiasm*?
3. Do you think of yourself as an enthusiastic person? Why or why not?

✓ **Reading with a Purpose**

B You are going to read an article about enthusiasm and how to become a more enthusiastic person. Write three questions you hope will be answered in the article.

1. _____

2. _____

3. _____

C Learn the meanings of the following words before you read the article.

awesome (2)	skeptical (5)	remarkably (17)
upbeat (3)	abundance (6)	agonize (21)
cynical (4)	prevailing (12)	
contagious (5)	persists (13)	

The E-Factor!

by Mary C. Hickey

1 Good news! We can all develop the quality that can make us happy, successful—even thin.

2 When I first met my friend Carol, I was convinced she was the luckiest woman alive. It seems like everything in her world is always wonderful. She describes her husband as "the greatest guy you could meet" and her job in real estate sales as "loads of fun." When she talks about places she's been or people she's met, she uses words like *awesome*, *fabulous*, and *terrific*.

3 But over the years, as I've gotten to know her better, I've realized that, really, Carol is no luckier than anyone else. Like all of us, she has her share of ups and downs. What is special about her, though, is her attitude: No matter what happens, Carol looks at the bright side. She somehow manages to remain upbeat, energetic, and vivacious. She is absolutely and totally . . . enthusiastic!

4 For a time, the cynical side of me found Carol's cheerful spirit a bit much. (I mean, really, how can anyone be happy all the time?) But more and more, I've grown to admire—even envy—this character trait. I've seen how Carol's enthusiasm works for her. She does well at her job, has lots of friends, and always seems to enjoy what she's doing.

5 What's more, I'm increasingly finding Carol delightful to be around. Her upbeat spirit is contagious, even for skeptical people like me. Whenever I'm with her, I can actually feel my own enthusiasm bubble to the surface. And, the fact is, that sure beats feeling cynical.

The Winning Edge

6 What's behind this E-factor, that magical quality called enthusiasm? Why do some people have it in abundance? And, most important, what can those of us who don't come by it naturally do to develop it?

7 Unfortunately, there are no hard-and-fast answers to these questions. Though researchers have long focused on negative emotions like depression and anxiety, it's only recently that psychologists have begun serious study of enthusiasm.

8 Already, though, scientists know enough to confirm what Norman Vincent Peale intuitively sensed back in 1952 when he first published his now-classic book, *The Power of Positive Thinking*. That is, that the character traits of enthusiastic people are typically associated with greater peace of mind, higher self-esteem, a stronger sense of well-being, and even better physical health and increased success in school and in the workplace.

9 "People who have a positive mental outlook have a distinct edge in life over others who are less enthusiastic," says psychiatrist Harold Bloomfield, M.D., coauthor of *The Power of 5* and numerous other top-selling books that teach, among other things, how to become more enthusiastic.

10 Indeed, the benefits of a positive outlook are wide ranging. C. R. Snyder, Ph.D., a professor of psychology at the University of Kansas, found that students who had positive expectations about their school performance actually performed better than those who didn't. In a study of college freshmen, Snyder and his colleagues discovered that the level of expectation among these students at the beginning of the semester was a better predictor of their grades than their high school grade point averages. And research on women on diets shows that those who maintained a positive outlook about their success were quicker to lose weight.

11 In fact, new research suggests that qualities like optimism and enthusiasm may actually somehow trigger our own immune systems[1] into working more effectively. A study of college students at the University of Michigan, for instance, found that pessimistic students were ill twice as many days as optimistic students and had four times as many doctors' visits over the course of a year.

An American Tradition

12 Yet, for all its positive values, enthusiasm isn't exactly in fashion these days. In fact, in a world characterized by chaos[2] and confusion, the prevailing mood seems to be one of suspicion and cynicism. A recent poll found that Americans' level of optimism about the future has been steadily declining.

13 But social observers say this may be a short-lived malaise[3]; the reality is that an upbeat spirit is deeply embedded in the American character. "There has always been a strain of positive optimism and enthusiasm in this country," notes Charles Bassett, Ph.D., professor of English and American studies at Colby College in Waterville, Maine. Adds Frank Farley, Ph.D., a psychologist at Temple University, "A spirit of enthusiasm persists in our culture today."

The Roots of Enthusiasm

14 What exactly is enthusiasm? Where does the trait come from? Why do some people, like my friend Carol, seem to be brimming with so much of the E-factor, while other people (myself included) can get enthusiastic about one thing and remain matter-of-fact about something else?

15 Experts believe a number of things are involved. Some say it's learned behavior that is either encouraged or quashed during childhood. But genetics may also play a role. "Some people seem to be born with a lot of joy juice," says Auke Tellegen, Ph.D., a professor of psychology at the University of Minnesota in Minneapolis, who has been researching a personality trait he calls "positive emotionality," a clinical term that is synonymous with *enthusiasm*.

16 According to Tellegen, research suggests that a person's level of positive emotionality may be related to heightened levels of a brain chemical called dopamine,

---

[1] **immune system** – the system by which your body protects itself from disease

[2] **chaos** – complete disorder

[3] **malaise** – a general feeling of anxiety, unhappiness, or dissatisfaction

though it is not clear exactly what causes this chemical to be produced in abundance. Some studies suggest that enthusiasm may also be an inherited trait. Tellegen cites research involving identical twins who, though raised in different families, typically share the same level of enthusiasm.

My Quest for Enthusiasm

17 But what happens if you haven't inherited the E-gene? Is it possible to raise your level of enthusiasm and live life a little more fully? Inspired by my friend Carol, I recently decided to find out. Not that I'd been particularly unhappy or anything, but my fortieth birthday was coming up, and I felt that it was time to start enjoying life more. So about six months ago, I made a conscious effort to try to be more enthusiastic about things, and, remarkably, it seems to be working.

18 How did I do it? I went to the library and borrowed an armload of self-help books and tapes by motivational speakers, and at a card store I found some posters and refrigerator magnets with such sentiments as "Attitude: It's a Small Word That Makes a Big Difference!" "When Life Hands You a Lemon, Make Lemonade!" and "Don't Sweat the Small Stuff. And Remember, It's All Small Stuff!"

19 Frankly, not all of it was for me (the more I listened to a tape on enthusiasm by one motivational speaker, for instance, the sillier it sounded). But at the same time, I did manage to find lots of good stuff.

20 I've become conscious of my tendency to think of excuses for why I can't do something instead of concentrating on why I can. For example, when a friend asked me to try in-line skating[4], I put aside my initial reaction (Are you kidding? I'll break my legs.) and forced myself to reconsider (If I can ice-skate, I'm sure I can do this, too.). I've been rolling along ever since— enthusiastically.

21 I've started giving myself little pep talks[5] whenever I find myself falling into a slump. On the bus on my way home from work, for example—a time when I'd normally agonize over my difficulties juggling a job, a house, and a family—I close my eyes and tell myself how lucky I am. I've got a fabulous home! An awesome job! A wonderful husband! And two of the most terrific kids in the world. (Honest, they are!)

22 No, I'll never be a bubbly spirit like my friend Carol. It's just not my style. And part of being enthusiastically upbeat, I've come to realize, is accepting yourself for who you are. But that doesn't mean it isn't possible to make some minor adjustments. The fact is that I have added a little more joy juice to my life—and if I can do it, anyone can. Now that's something to get really enthusiastic about!

---

[4] **in-line skating** – moving on skates that have a single row of wheels under each skate

[5] **pep talk** – a speech that is intended to encourage people to try harder.

Intro

Benefits

what people are like

Comprehension Check

Circle the letter of the choice that best completes the sentence or answers the question.

1. Which sentence best expresses the main point of the article?
    a. Students who have a positive attitude perform better in school.
    b. Enthusiasm is basically an inherited trait that is difficult to alter.
    c. Developing a more enthusiastic attitude can make you happier and more successful.
    d. Enthusiasm is something you cannot acquire at any time.

2. The author's feelings about Carol have _____.
    a. changed over time
    b. remained the same
    c. become more negative
    d. faded over the years

3. According to a study at the University of Michigan, _____.
    a. pessimistic students were sick more often than optimistic students
    b. optimistic students had four times as many doctors' visits as pessimistic students
    c. optimistic and pessimistic students were ill the same number of times
    d. pessimistic students rarely got sick compared to optimistic students

4. The author thinks her friend Carol _____.
    a. is the luckiest person in the world
    b. needs more luck in her life
    c. is no luckier than anyone else
    d. has had a lot of bad luck

5. Which statement would the author agree with?
    a. We live in a confusing world where most people are cynical and suspicious.
    b. The world today is so safe that people are generally trusting and secure.
    c. Most people are envious of others because our world is so competitive.
    d. Because our world is chaotic, people are becoming increasingly optimistic.

6. According to a recent survey, the number of people who feel the American Dream is still alive _____.
   a. is increasing
   b. has remained the same
   c. is decreasing
   d. is unpredictable

7. The author believes that _____.
   a. it is impossible to become a more enthusiastic person
   b. there is no reason to change your level of enthusiasm
   c. it is possible to train yourself to become more enthusiastic
   d. motivational tapes are the best way to become more enthusiastic

8. According to the article, which of the following are involved in a person's level of enthusiasm?
   a. genetics
   b. learned behavior in childhood
   c. heightened levels of dopamine
   d. all of the above

9. The article mentions research that has been done on all of the following EXCEPT _____.
   a. the relationship between optimism and enthusiasm and our immune system
   b. the effect of a positive outlook on women who are dieting
   c. the effects of enthusiasm on job performance
   d. the correlation between positive outlook and performance in school

10. Research involving identical twins who were raised apart but shared the same level of enthusiasm was cited to support the idea that

    _____.
    a. enthusiasm is a learned behavior
    b. identical twins raised apart are less enthusiastic than those raised together
    c. identical twins share the same level of enthusiasm as the general population
    d. enthusiasm may be an inherited trait

A Cross out the word in each group that does not belong.

1. fabulous   predictable   awesome   terrific

2. worry   agonize   struggle   fascinate

3. remarkably   amazingly   surprisingly   generally

4. abundance   scarcity   wealth   plenty

5. persevere   give up   keep on   persist

6. suspicious   cynical   skeptical   bubbly

7. depressed   vivacious   upbeat   energetic

8. general   widespread   singular   prevailing

9. infectious   contagious   catching   believable

B Circle the correct answer.

1. Which decision would you be more likely to <u>agonize</u> over?
   a. which job to take   b. what to have for dinner

2. If you stop to admire the <u>awesome</u> scenery, you think it is _____.
   a. boring   b. fabulous

3. A <u>remarkably</u> noisy place is _____.
   a. not very noisy   b. surprisingly noisy

4. If you have an <u>abundance</u> of paper, you have _____.
   a. more than enough   b. too little

5. If someone <u>persists</u> in asking you questions, he _____.
   a. continues to ask you questions   b. decides to stop questioning you

6. A <u>skeptical</u> person _____.
   a. believes everything she hears   b. often doubts what she hears

7. A person who is usually <u>upbeat</u> is often in a _____.
   a. good mood   b. bad mood

8. If the <u>prevailing</u> view is that the economy is going to improve, _____.
   a. few people think it is going to get better   b. most people expect it to get better

9. When someone's laughter is <u>contagious</u>, _____.
   a. other people laugh, too   b. no one else laughs

10. If you are <u>cynical</u> about the mayor's promises, you think _____.
    a. he is sincere   b. he is not sincere

SKILL FOR SUCCESS

Understanding Word Parts: The Suffix -*some*

In this chapter, you learned the meaning of *awesome*. The suffix -*some* can be added to other words to mean "characterized by some specific condition or quality." It can also be added to some numbers to mean "a group of a specified number of members." For example, *foursome* means "a group of four people."

C Match each word with the correct definition.

Word	Definition
_____ **1.** lonesome	**a.** healthy
_____ **2.** twosome	**b.** awkward because of being large, heavy
_____ **3.** tiresome	**c.** boring or annoying
_____ **4.** wholesome	**d.** causing problems
_____ **5.** troublesome	**e.** lonely
_____ **6.** cumbersome	**f.** a group of two people

D Complete each sentence with the correct word from Exercise C.

1. Sue and Ed are always together. They've become a real
   _____.

2. Can you help me carry this trunk? It's really big and
   _____.

3. I try to eat fresh _____ foods like fruits and vegetables.

4. I'm so _____ since you moved away. I really miss you.

5. This movie is very long, and the music is boring and
   _____.

6. The fact that there is no evidence is _____. The police can't solve the crime.

Talk It Over

Discuss these questions as a class.

The author mentioned posters and refrigerator magnets with these sayings. Discuss what you think each saying means.

1. "Attitude: It's a small word that makes a big difference!"
2. "When life hands you a lemon, make lemonade."
3. "Don't sweat the small stuff. And remember, it's all small stuff!"

Chapter 1   **43**

CHAPTER **2**

Happiness Is . . .

Before You Read

A Discuss these questions with a partner.

1. What kinds of things do you think make most people happy?
2. Can you think of a time in your life when you were very happy? Describe that time to your partner.
3. Would you describe yourself as a happy person? Why or why not?

B Learn the meanings of the following words before you read the article.

illustrious (1)	illusions (4)	perpetual (9)
no-brainer (1)	trite (5)	brilliant (10)
misguided (1)	modest (5)	
fluctuate (3)	adversity (6)	

Happiness Is . . .

by Andrea Sachs

1   Why would an illustrious professor of psychology at Harvard decide to study a subject like happiness? That's a no-brainer for Dr. Daniel Gilbert, the author of *Stumbling on Happiness*, a fascinating book that explores our sometimes misguided attempts to find happiness. "Why would anybody study anything else?" asks Gilbert. "Something close to 100 percent of all human behavior is directed in one way or the other toward attaining happiness. In some sense, this is the goal of most of our actions. So it seems like the obvious thing for a psychologist to study."

2   **Andrea Sachs:** Is the desire for happiness wired into[1] our psyche[2]?

   Dr. Daniel Gilbert: I would go further than that. I'd say the phrase "desire for

---

[1] **wired into** – built into; a natural part of

[2] **psyche** – someone's mind or basic nature that controls how he or she thinks or behaves

Daniel Gilbert is a psychology professor at Harvard University. One of his areas of research is happiness.

happiness" is redundant, because it's what desire means. What could it mean to desire something except to believe that it will increase your happiness? That's why it seems odd if somebody says, "desire a punch in the mouth." We can't figure out why they would desire it. A punch in the mouth doesn't lead to happiness, so how could you really want it?

3 **AS:** Does our level of happiness fluctuate?

DG: It certainly does. The world conspires to decrease our level of happiness; we fight back by trying to increase it. Human life can be seen as the struggle between these two forces.

4 **AS:** Why are we often so poor at predicting what will make us happy?

DG: Just as we are prone to illusions of memory and perception, so are we prone to illusions of imagination. We don't realize how much imagination puts in and leaves out, how much the imagined future is influenced by the actual present, and how differently we will think about the future once it happens.

5 **AS:** There's a whole self-help literature about how to be happy. Do any of those books hit it on the mark?

DG: You might be surprised to hear me say that I think the books are largely right. Most of the advice that you get in books on how to be happy is extremely trite and well-worn— trite and well-worn because it's true. The problem is, it's not a magic bullet[3]. What we want—as Americans especially, but as human beings in general—is to open a book and find that there's something we've been missing, that happiness is really to be found—Oh, my gosh! we slap our heads!—by putting on a green hat, standing on one leg, and singing the National Anthem[4]. If only we knew this were it, we would have done it long ago. But if you open these books, what are they largely going to tell you? Two things that psychologists and economists have confirmed scientifically have been shouted from mountaintops for thousands of years by wise people. First, the pursuit of material possessions[5] has a very modest and complicated relationship to happiness. Second, social relationships have an extremely powerful and simple relation to happiness.

6 **AS:** When does money make people happy?

DG: When it moves them out of poverty and into the middle class[6]. There's an enormous difference in your happiness if you earn $10,000 or $50,000. That extra money is buying you out of poor health, poverty, adversity, worrying about where your next meal will come from, worrying about your children's future and safety. However, once people are earning enough to be in the middle class, more money doesn't make them much happier. So the difference between earning $10,000 and earning $50,000 is much bigger

[3] **magic bullet** – an instant cure

[4] **National Anthem** – a country's official song, which is played on public occasions

[5] **material possessions** – things you own

[6] **middle class** – the people in a society who are neither very rich nor poor

in terms of happiness than the difference between earning $100,000 and earning a million.

7 **AS:** The average person wouldn't believe that, would they?

DG: No. But data are stunningly clear. You can graph this again and again, and there are economists who do. The way I try to explain this to people is to say, "Forget about money. Let's talk about pancakes. Do you think you get happy when you eat a pancake?" Everyone says, "Sure, pancakes are delicious." Do two make you happier than one? "You bet! I like to have two." But once we get up to six or seven, people start rubbing their stomachs and realizing they're getting full. The tenth pancake doesn't make you happier than the ninth one did, which made you only a little happier than the eighth one did. People understand with something like food, we reach a point of satiety[7]. It turns out it's exactly the same way with money.

8 **AS:** Why don't the same things make everyone happy?

DG: I actually think the same things do make most people happy. The differences are extremely small, and around the margins. You like peach ice cream; I like strawberry ice cream. Both of us like ice cream much better than a smack on the head. If you look at the whole world of possible things that we could experience, you'll notice that almost all human beings want the same stuff, and almost all human beings want to avoid the same stuff. I think it's an illusion that we are remarkably different.

9 **AS:** Does happiness ever get boring, like a perpetually sunny day?

DG: I think in some ways, by definition, it couldn't. Because if you were bored, then you wouldn't be happy. But if you're asking a question about whether we can and should want to have perpetual happiness, the answer to the second question is moot[8], because the answer to the first question is no. It's not possible to be in precisely the same positive emotional state at all times. Emotions are the brain's way of telling us that we're doing something that's good or bad for us in the evolutionary sense. Think of emotions as a compass; they're there to guide us in the right direction. What good is a compass that's always stuck on north? Your emotions are meant to fluctuate, just like your blood pressure is meant to fluctuate. It's a system that's supposed to move back and forth, between happy and unhappy. That's how the system guides you through the world.

10 **AS:** Would you describe yourself as happy?

DG: Extremely. I have everything that I could possibly want in life, from a gorgeous granddaughter and a wonderful wife, brilliant students, the best job anyone could hope for, and about half of my hair. Not the half I would have kept, but no one consulted me.

---

[7] **satiety** – feeling full

[8] **moot** – no longer likely to happen or no longer important

Comprehension Check

A Read these statements. If a statement is true according to the article, write *T* on the line. If it is false, write *F*.

_____ 1. The article supports the conclusion that our level of happiness always remains the same.

_____ 2. Most people, according to Gilbert, have illusions of memory, perception, and imagination.

_____ 3. Gilbert does not think there is a relationship between happiness and social relationships.

_____ 4. Daniel Gilbert believes that the same kinds of things make most people happy.

_____ 5. According to Gilbert, our emotions help guide us in the right direction.

_____ 6. Gilbert thinks that once people are earning enough money to be in the middle class, making more money won't lead to much more happiness.

_____ 7. Gilbert advises people to put on a green hat and stand on one leg to increase their level of happiness.

SKILL FOR SUCCESS

Paraphrasing

Paraphrasing is a way of using your own words to express something you have read. The purpose is to restate the original information in a simpler form to make the meaning clearer to you. Paraphrasing will help you understand difficult sentences more easily.

B Paraphrase the following passages from the article. Your paraphrase should express the main idea of the original sentence as clearly and simply as possible. There is more than one way to paraphrase each passage from the original interview. See the example below.

Original: Two things that psychologists and economists have confirmed scientifically have been shouted from mountaintops for thousands of years by wise people. First, the pursuit of material possessions has a very modest and complicated relationship to happiness. Second, social relationships have an extremely powerful and simple relation to happiness.

Paraphrase: Psychologists and economists have proven what wise people already knew: that material possessions have a smaller and more complex relationship to happiness than social relationships do.

OR

People have long believed that social relationships have a stronger and simpler relation to happiness than the quest for material possessions. Psychologists and economists have proven it scientifically.

OR

Scientists have proven that the relationship between material possessions and happiness is not as strong and simple as the relationship between happiness and social relationships. This is something wise people already knew.

1. If you look at the whole world of possible things that we could experience, you'll notice that almost all human beings want the same stuff, and almost all human beings want to avoid the same stuff. I think it's an illusion that we are remarkably different.

   _____

   _____

   _____

2. Emotions are the brain's way of telling us that we're doing something that's good or bad for us in the evolutionary sense. Think of emotions as a compass; they're there to guide us in the right direction. What good is a compass that's always stuck on north? Your emotions are meant to fluctuate, just like your blood pressure is meant to fluctuate.

   _____

   _____

   _____

3. There's an enormous difference in your happiness if you earn $10,000 or $50,000. That extra money is buying you out of poor health, poverty, adversity, worrying about where your next meal will come from, worrying about your children's future and safety. However, once people are earning enough to be in the middle class, more money doesn't make them much happier.

   _____

   _____

   _____

Vocabulary Practice

A Choose the word or phrase that is closest in meaning to the underlined word in each sentence.

1. Several <u>illustrious</u> economists will be speaking at the conference.
   a. young and untraditional
   b. famous and well-respected
   c. intelligent but unknown

2. Most of the questions on the exam were difficult, but the last one was a <u>no-brainer</u>.
   a. something easy to understand and do
   b. the most difficult thing
   c. something very confusing

3. He made a <u>misguided</u> attempt to resolve the problem.
   a. successful because it was based on good judgment
   b. very wise and helpful because it was simple
   c. unsuccessful because it was based on bad judgment

4. It's hard for Maria to save money because her income is <u>modest</u>.
   a. not large
   b. very large
   c. unpredictable

5. He shows great courage even in times of <u>adversity</u>.
   a. good health
   b. freedom and opportunity
   c. difficulties and problems

6. He accepted the job under the <u>illusion</u> that it was safe.
   a. false idea
   b. truth
   c. hope

7. The amount of rain <u>fluctuates</u> from between 30 and 42 inches per year.
   a. doesn't change
   b. changes often
   c. keeps increasing

8. The politician made the usual <u>trite</u> comments about improving the economy.
   a. common and overused
   b. new and exciting
   c. complicated and hard to understand

9. My sister thinks all three of her children are beautiful and <u>brilliant</u>.
   a. good-looking
   b. very intelligent
   c. well-behaved

10. The children live in <u>perpetual</u> fear of being punished.
    a. continual
    b. recent
    c. mild

B Cross out the word in each group that does not belong.

1. illustrious   distinguished   famous   unknown
2. no-brainer   complication   difficulty   confusion
3. misguided   wise   foolish   mistaken
4. modest   moderate   small   excessive
5. adversity   privilege   hardship   difficulty
6. truth   certainty   actuality   illusion
7. fluctuate   vary   persist   change
8. common   trite   unoriginal   exciting
9. intelligent   stupid   brilliant   smart
10. continuous   lasting   fleeting   perpetual

SKILL FOR SUCCESS

Understanding Word Parts: The Prefix *mis-*
A **prefix** is a letter or group of letters added to the beginning of a word to change its meaning. When the prefix *mis-* is added to a word, it means "a *bad* or *wrong* action." In the article, you learned the word *misguided*.

C Write a definition for each word. Use your dictionary to help you.

1. mistrust _____
2. misbehave _____
3. miscalculate _____
4. miscount _____
5. mishandle _____
6. misrepresent _____

D Complete each sentence with the correct word from Exercise C. Be sure to use the correct form of the words.

1. I think the police completely _____ the investigation.

2. I hope the children don't _____ while I'm gone.

3. I thought I had five stamps left, but I only have four. I must have _____ .

4. Don't marry John if you _____ him.

5. The article not only misquoted me but also _____ my views on the environment.

6. We didn't have enough food at the party. I _____ the amount of food that people would eat.

Discuss these questions as a class.

1. What do you think is the most important factor in making you a happy person?
2. Do you disagree with any of Gilbert's ideas? Which ones?
3. Do your emotions fluctuate a lot in one day?

How Color Can Change Your Life

Before You Read

A Discuss these questions with a partner.

1. What is your favorite color? What is your least favorite color?
2. Do you associate any color with happiness? How about sadness?
3. Do you think the color of a room can affect your mood? How?

✓ **Previewing and Predicting**

B Preview the article and then make predictions by checking (✔) the topics you think will be discussed.

☐ 1. How colors can affect your eating habits
☐ 2. Why countries pick certain colors for their flags
☐ 3. The ways colors can affect what people think about you
☐ 4. How your mood can be influenced by colors
☐ 5. How artists choose colors for their paintings
☐ 6. The relationship between stress and colors
☐ 7. How our eyes see color

C Learn the meanings of the following words and phrase before you read the article.

pastels (4)   stick to (7)   irritable (9)
turmoil (5)   wardrobe (9)   savvy (10)

How Color Can Change Your Life

by Pamela Stock

1 It's hard to imagine a world without color. Colors bring beauty into our lives and influence the way we behave. Some people even think certain colors can make you happy! As you will see, colors affect your life in many ways.

Increasing Energy

2 Suppose you have been working all day. You are very tired and you can barely keep your eyes open. There could be a simple explanation for your low energy level. There's not enough bright blue in your life. Color experts say that people are more productive when they work in blue rooms. So decorate your walls with lots of bright blue artwork: It could help you stay energized.

3 There have been several interesting studies on the positive effects of the color blue. For example, a study conducted at the University of California at Berkeley showed that people could lift weights longer when they faced a blue poster board than when they faced a pink one. And the color blue might even make you better at certain sports. Scientists at the University of Texas at Austin found that when athletes looked at a blue light, their hand–eye coordination[1] improved.

Beating Stress

4 If it's 2:00 A.M. and you still can't sleep because you're stressed out over things

that happened at work, think pastels. Pink and light blue walls have been shown to lower blood pressure and heart rates, says health writer Morton Walker, author of *The Power of Color*. Try hanging up pink or pale blue curtains in your bedroom. It could make you feel calmer.

5 Pastels are not the only colors that can calm you down. If you're feeling really stressed, you may find yourself turning to shades of green. Because it is the easiest color for the eye to process, people who have turmoil in their lives often choose green accessories or housewares, says Cynthia Cornell. Cornell works for the Wagner Institute for Color Research, a marketing research firm that tracks color trends and performs studies for corporate clients such as Sears, Ford, and Pratt and Lambert Paint. "Those who are drawn to green are often in search of security," she

[1] **hand–eye coordination** – the ability to use information received through your eyes to guide your hands in an activity such as writing or catching a ball

says. Think of it this way: Adding a green pillow is a quick, inexpensive, and attractive fix.

Eating Well

6 If you're eating everything in sight, you should be on the alert—red alert, that is. In other words, stay away from red. Studies prove that the color red is a stimulant that affects your appetite. When you see red, your body produces a chemical called adrenaline that increases your heart rate and enhances your appetite, says Walker. Some fast-food restaurants paint their walls bright red to encourage people to eat quickly and leave, according to Cornell. That way, the restaurants can serve more people.

7 If you can't stick to a diet, you may want to use a blue color scheme. Research shows that blue reduces appetite, possibly because so few blue foods exist in nature, suggests Walker. In addition, market research shows that people associate blue (and green) with mold.

Getting Promoted

8 Suppose you are starting a new job, and you've decided to wear your bright red suit so people will notice you. Stop and think again. You might not be sending the proper message. While small amounts of red—such as a scarf or blouse—can be warm and inviting, too much can be overwhelming. Instead, wear something blue. In the United States, dark blue has historically been associated with power, responsibility, and respectability.

9 For contrast, you might add a small amount of yellow to your wardrobe. Yellow is the first color that your eye processes, color researchers have discovered. That's why stores use yellow signs to mark sale items. But yellow, like red, is best in small amounts. Too much of these colors can make people irritable.

10 Keep in mind that color awareness won't make you master of the universe. And you certainly shouldn't feel you have to give up your personal preferences in order to become a savvy color strategist. But remember, color can make a difference. ■

After You Read

Comprehension Check

A Answer these questions.

1. What color enhances the appetite? Why?
2. What color is the easiest for the eye to process?
3. What color do stores use to indicate sale items? Why?
4. What color reduces the appetite? Why?
5. How should you use red in your wardrobe for work?
6. What is the color dark blue associated with in the United States?

Making Inferences

An *inference* is a reasonable conclusion that you make based on information provided in the text. It is an educated guess. Because authors do not always state information directly, good readers need to **make inferences** while they are reading. To make inferences, you should combine information suggested in the reading with information you already know.

SKILL FOR SUCCESS ✔

F Y I

Color blindness affects more men than women. Eight out of every 100 men are color blind, whereas only one out of every 200 women is color blind.

B Check (✔) the statements that are inferences you can make based on the information in the reading and what you already know. Discuss your answers with a partner.

❑ 1. A red suit with a blue tie would be a better choice for a job interview than a blue suit with a red tie.

❑ 2. If your job is very stressful, light blue would be a good color to choose for your walls.

❑ 3. Pastels are the only colors that are comforting.

❑ 4. The colors you wear can send important messages to others.

❑ 5. If you want to lose weight, it would not be a good idea to use a lot of red when you decorate your kitchen.

❑ 6. If you have trouble staying awake and concentrating on your work, try moving to a place with lots of bright blue.

❑ 7. Color awareness is the most important ingredient for success on the job.

✔ **Summarizing**

C Using your own words, write a one-paragraph summary of the article.

_____

_____

_____

_____

_____

_____

Vocabulary Practice

A Circle the correct answer.

1. Which is an example of a <u>pastel</u>?
   a. light blue   b. bright red

2. Which could cause <u>turmoil</u> in someone's life?
   a. getting fired from a job   b. getting a good grade on a test

3. If you <u>stick to</u> a promise, you _____.
   a. break it   **b.** keep it

4. Which is an example of something in a person's <u>wardrobe</u>?
   a. books   **b.** suits

5. If your friend is in an <u>irritable</u> mood, you would probably _____.
   a. want to spend time with her   **b.** want to stay away from her

6. If you think someone has decorating <u>savvy</u>, you _____.
   a. would ask him for advice when you redecorate your office
   b. wouldn't want his decorating opinion

SKILL FOR SUCCESS

Learning Idioms: Expressions about Color
An **idiom** is a group of words that has a special meaning. The meaning of the group of words as a whole is different from the meanings of the individual words. Many idioms in English are related to color. For example, if something happens *out of the blue*, it happens suddenly and you are not expecting it. Learning idioms is an important part of learning a new language and will help you become a more fluent reader.

B Study the meanings of these idioms. Then complete the sentences. Be sure to use the correct form of the word.

- *Paint the town red* means "to go out and enjoy yourself, usually in order to celebrate something."
- Someone who has *a green thumb* is good at keeping plants healthy.
- If you *don't have a red cent*, you have no money.
- *Green with envy* means "very envious of someone."
- *A little white lie* is a lie that you tell in order not to upset someone.
- *Roll out the red carpet* means "to give an important person a special welcome."
- *Give someone the green light* means "to give permission for someone to do something."
- If you talk until you are *blue in the face*, you say the same thing over and over but people don't pay attention to what you say.

1. After staying inside and studying for final exams for three weeks, we decided to go out and ___*paint the town red*___ when our last exam was over.

2. We _____ for the president of our college when he came to our house for dinner.

3. I can't go to the movies with you tonight. I'm so broke, I _____.

4. After saying no for two days, my parents finally
_____ to go on the camping trip.

5. Alice was _____ when she saw her best friend's
beautiful engagement ring.

6. My grandmother always has the most beautiful garden in town.
Everyone says she has _____.

7. Although Dave didn't like his wife's new haircut, he told
_____ and said that he loved it.

8. Antonio argued with his parents until he was
_____, but they still wouldn't let him borrow
their car for the weekend.

C Do you have any idiomatic expressions related to color in your language?
If so, give some examples.

Choose a Title

Read the article below and choose the best title for it. Write the title on
the line.

1. Colors in Our Environment
2. Geomancers: The Masters of Feng Shui
3. Achieving Health, Happiness, and Success with Feng Shui
4. The Role of Common Sense in Feng Shui

_____

Color isn't the only thing in our environment that can affect our moods. Some people also believe that the way things are arranged can help us achieve happiness.

Feng shui is the ancient Asian art of arranging your environment, be it home or workplace, to achieve health, happiness, and success. Invented more than 5,000 years ago in China, it has been practiced for centuries in many Eastern cultures and has gained interest among Westerners as well.

Feng shui is based on the principle that by balancing the earth's natural forces, we can tap into chi (good energy) and achieve harmony and good luck. Masters of the art of feng shui are called geomancers. They can measure a building's ability to attract good luck based on its design, shape, orientation, layout, and location. Every building has its own harmony, and it is the role of the geomancer to bring good energy into the building. In this way, they try to increase the happiness and success of its inhabitants. Because space greatly affects our sense of comfort and well-being, geomancers also advise clients where to place furniture and other objects in a room as well as what colors, patterns, and textures to use in furnishings.

The message here is that if things are not going well, look at your environment. For example, if your back is to a door when you are sitting at your desk, you might want to rearrange your room. It's unsettling when you can't see who is coming through the door. Remember: Common sense has a role in feng shui, too.

Talk It Over

F Y I

Today, banks, hotels, houses, and even new communities have been planned using feng shui principles.

Discuss these questions as a class.

1. The way we feel about different colors is influenced by our culture. What does each of the following colors mean in your culture?

black	green	white
blue	red	yellow

2. Does the placement of furniture and other objects in your home affect how you feel and your level of comfort? If so, give some examples.

Tie It All Together

Discussion

Discuss these questions in a small group.

1. Do you think it's possible to change a major characteristic of your personality? Is it really possible to become more enthusiastic?
2. What do you think are the most important ingredients of happiness?
3. Many people find that exercising puts them in a better mood. Do you feel better when you exercise? How does exercise affect your mood?
4. Do you listen to music to lift your spirits? What kind of music do you find helps your mood?
5. Who do you usually talk to when you are upset about something? What does this person do that helps? Do you ever help others when they feel upset?
6. Discuss these quotes.
   a. Enthusiasm releases the drive to carry you over obstacles and adds significance to all you do. (Norman Vincent Peale)
   b. There are as many nights as days, and the one is just as long as the other in the year's course. Even a happy life cannot be without a measure of darkness, and the word *happy* would lose its meaning if it were not balanced by sadness. (Carl Jung)
   c. The best way to cheer yourself up is to try to cheer somebody else up. (Mark Twain)
   d. When one door of happiness closes, another opens: but often we look so long at the closed door that we do not see the one which has been opened for us. (Helen Keller)

Complete the crossword puzzle with words from the unit.

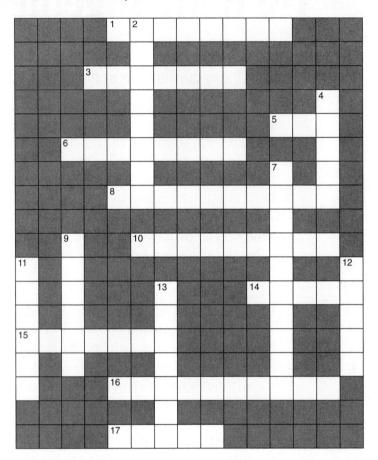

ACROSS

1. Make a mistake when counting something

3. A psychology professor at Harvard University

5. A color that enhances appetite

6. "It's a small word that makes a big difference!"

8. The "E-factor" describes it

10. Very intelligent

14. Color of a lie you tell not to upset someone

15. A pair of people

16. Masters of feng shui

17. ___ with envy

DOWN

2. A false idea

4. A group of words that has a special meaning

7. Restate information in your own words

9. The first color that your eye processes

11. A soft, pale color

12. Author of *The Power of Positive Thinking*

13. A synonym for *fabulous*

How to Be Happy

Think about the articles you have read and the ideas you have discussed in Unit 2. Do you believe that happiness is something predetermined in our genes? How much control do you think we have over our happiness?

A Study these words. Then watch the video.

exuberant	irrepressibly	tendency
fearfulness	irritability	thermostat
genetic blueprint	MRIs	thieves
grumpy	raised	vibes

B All of the statements below are false. Read the statements and then watch the video again. Rewrite each statement to make it true. Add a detail from the video if you can.

1. Dr. Lykken's study found that identical twins have very different happiness scores.

   Dr. Lykken's study found that identical twins have very similar happiness scores. This supports the idea that happiness is genetic.

2. Nathan Fox's brain scans, called MRIs, show that children must learn from their parents how to be happy.

   _____

   _____

   _____

3. According to Dr. Lykken's thermostat analogy, a low setting means we are always cheerful and a high setting means we are always grumpy.

   _____

   _____

   _____

4. Dr. Lykken believes we have no control over our level of happiness and that it is completely determined by our genes.

   _____

   _____

   _____

5. According to Dr. Lykken, the recipe for happiness is depending on life's big pleasures like winning the lottery.

   _____

   _____

   _____

C Discuss this question with a partner or in a small group.

You have a friend who is always grumpy and irritable. Based on your own beliefs or some ideas from the video, what advice would you give your friend about how he or she could be happier?

Reader's Journal

Think about the topics and ideas you have read about and discussed in this unit. Pick a topic from the following list, choose one of the discussion questions in the unit, or write about an idea of your own. Write about it for ten to twenty minutes.

- ways to get into a good mood/ways to get out of a bad mood
- the moodiest person you know
- how colors influence your life
- the most enthusiastic person you know

Vocabulary Self-Test

Complete each sentence with the correct word or phrase.

A
adversity	illustrious	prevailing
awesome	misguided	remarkably
fluctuate	persists	skeptical

1. They were _____ calm after the car accident.

2. The movie is _____. You should see it right away.

3. I am _____ about her ability to do the job. She doesn't have much experience.

4. The _____ attitude among experts is that the economy will continue to _____ between periods of growth and periods of decline.

5. The company's business plan was _____, and it lost a lot of money.

6. If your toothache _____ for much longer, you should call a dentist.

7. We are honored to have Dr. Singh, the _____ professor of neurology, speak at the conference.

8. There's an old but wise saying: "The road to happiness is paved with _____." This means you will encounter difficulties and hard times on your way to achieving happiness.

B
brilliant	perpetual	turmoil
irritable	savvy	wardrobe
pastel	stick to	

1. What a(n) _____ idea! Let's do it!

2. She is a(n) _____ businesswoman. She has great judgment, and her company is doing very well.

3. Please _____ the plan, and we'll finish the job sooner.

4. I think you need to add more _____ colors to your _____.

5. You've been _____ all day. What's the matter? Are you upset about something?

6. The office has been in _____ ever since the manager quit.

7. My sister is always happy. She has a(n) _____ smile on her face.

C abundance cynical no-brainer
agonized illusion trite
contagious modest upbeat

1. There's nothing new in this essay. All the ideas are _____ and common.

2. We were hoping the new movie would be a big hit, but it had only _____ success.

3. I like being around Janice. She's _____ and fun to be with.

4. We have a(n) _____ of children's books. Please take some for your kids.

5. She _____ over the decision of whether or not to marry Kevin. In the end, she decided not to.

6. Why are you so _____? You should try to be more trusting of people you meet.

7. Everyone got the answer to the question right. It was a(n) _____.

8. Stay away from Peter. He's got a(n) _____ eye infection.

9. Mr. Dole looked like a rich man, but it was just a(n) _____. He borrowed the expensive suit he was wearing from his brother. In reality, he doesn't have a red cent.

HOME AND FAMILY

Few people would argue that home and family are two of the most important factors in shaping our lives. If you are like most people, you have strong feelings about your place in your family, the house you grew up in, and the place you consider your hometown. As you read the selections in this unit, think about your feelings about your own home and family.

Points to Ponder

Think about these questions and discuss them in a small group.

1. What memories do you have about the place where you grew up?
2. Do you like the place where you are living now? Why or why not?
3. How many siblings (brothers and sisters) do you have? Who is the eldest child in your family? Who is the youngest?

The House on Mango Street

Before You Read

A Discuss these questions with a partner.

1. How many different houses or apartments have you lived in? Which one did you like the best? Why? Which one did you like the least? Why?
2. What do you like about your home? What don't you like?
3. If you could change anything about your present home, what would you change?

B Learn the meanings of the following words and phrases before you read the story.

landlord (2)   crumbling (5)   Laundromat (6)

dreamed up (4)   swollen (5)   for the time being (11)

Sandra Cisneros is a best-selling author whose stories draw on her Latino heritage. One of her most famous books is *The House on Mango Street*. The book is a series of stories about the life of Esperanza, a Mexican-American girl. In this story, Esperanza writes about the move with her family into a house on Mango Street.

The House on Mango Street

by Sandra Cisneros

1   We didn't always live on Mango Street. Before that we lived on Loomis on the third floor, and before that we lived on Keeler. Before Keeler it was Paulina, and before that I can't remember. But what I remember most is moving a lot. Each time it seemed there'd be one more of us. By the time we got to Mango Street we were six— Mama, Papa, Carlos, Kiki, my sister Nenny, and me.

2   The house on Mango Street is ours, and we don't have to pay rent to anybody, or share the yard with the people downstairs, or be careful not to make too much noise, and there isn't a landlord banging[1] on the ceiling with a broom. But even so, it's not the house we'd thought we'd get.

3   We had to leave the flat[2] on Loomis quick. The water pipes broke and the landlord wouldn't fix them because the house was too old. We had to leave fast. We were using the washroom next door and carrying water over in empty milk gallons. That's why Mama and Papa looked for a house, and that's why we moved into the house on Mango Street, far away, on the other side of town.

4   They always told us that one day we would move into a house, a real house that would be ours for always so we wouldn't have to move each year. And our house would have running water and pipes that worked. And inside it would have real stairs, not hallway stairs, but stairs inside like the houses on TV. And we'd have a basement and at least three washrooms so when we took a bath we wouldn't have to tell everybody. Our house would be white with trees around it, a great big yard and grass growing without a fence. This was the house Papa talked about when he held a lottery ticket, and this was the house Mama dreamed up in the stories she told us before we went to bed.

5   But the house on Mango Street is not the way they told it at all. It's small and red with tight steps in front and windows so small you'd think they were holding their breath. Bricks are crumbling in places, and the front door is so swollen you have to push hard to get in. There is no front yard, only four little elms[3] the city planted by the curb. Out back is a small garage for the car we don't own yet and a small yard that looks smaller between the two buildings on either side. There are stairs in our house, but they're ordinary hallway stairs, and the house has only one washroom. Everybody has to share a bedroom—Mama and Papa, Carlos and Kiki, me and Nenny.

---

[1] **bang** – to make a loud noise by hitting something against something hard

[2] **flat** – apartment

[3] **elm** – a large tree

6 Once when we were living on Loomis, a nun[4] from my school passed by and saw me playing out front. The Laundromat downstairs had been boarded up[5] because it had been robbed two days before and the owner had painted on the wood YES WE'RE OPEN so as not to lose business.

7 Where do you live? she asked.

8 There, I said pointing up to the third floor.

9 You live *there*?

10 *There*. I had to look to where she pointed—the third floor, the paint peeling[6], wooden bars Papa had nailed on the windows so we wouldn't fall out. You live *there*? The way she said it made me feel like nothing. *There*. I lived *there*. I nodded.

11 I knew then I had to have a house. A real house. One I could point to. But this isn't it. The house on Mango Street isn't it. For the time being, Mama says. Temporary, says Papa. But I know how those things go. ■

[4] **nun** – a member of a group of Catholic women who devote their lives to religion

[5] **boarded up** – covered with flat pieces of wood

[6] **peel** – to come off in small, thin pieces

After You Read

Comprehension Check

A Circle the correct answer.

1. When Esperanza describes the house on Mango Street, she sounds _____.
   a. disappointed
   b. afraid
   c. proud
   d. happy

2. Esperanza mentions _____.
   a. only one place where her family lived
   b. several other places where her family lived
   c. where her grandparents live
   d. where her family plans to move

3. Why did the family move from Loomis Street?
   a. They couldn't pay the rent.
   b. Their house was robbed.
   c. The water pipes broke.
   d. They won the lottery.

4. In describing the house on Mango Street, which of the following does the author NOT mention?
   a. the kitchen
   b. the stairs
   c. the windows
   d. the front door

5. The parents told the children _____.
   a. moving was fun and they would move every year
   b. they would move back into the house on Loomis Street
   c. they would buy a real house so they wouldn't have to move each year
   d. they would buy a house with one bedroom and one bathroom

✓ **Making Inferences**

B Check (✔) the statements that are inferences you can make based on the information in the story. Discuss your answers with a partner.

- ☐ 1. The family didn't like to move from place to place.
- ☐ 2. Esperanza was ashamed of the place where she lived on Loomis Street.
- ☐ 3. Esperanza doesn't believe that the house on Mango Street is temporary.
- ☐ 4. The owner of the Laundromat lived in the same building as Esperanza's family.
- ☐ 5. Esperanza's family eventually moved to a white house with trees and a backyard.
- ☐ 6. Esperanza's parents enjoyed lying to their children.
- ☐ 7. Esperanza's family didn't have a lot of money.
- ☐ 8. In the past, Esperanza's family had to be careful not to make too much noise.

Vocabulary Practice

A Match each word or phrase with the correct definition.

Word or Phrase	Definition
_____ 1. swollen	a. a place with washing machines where you pay to do your laundry
_____ 2. landlord	
_____ 3. dream up	b. breaking into small pieces
_____ 4. crumbling	c. larger than usual
_____ 5. Laundromat	d. now
_____ 6. for the time being	e. a person who owns a building that people pay to use
	f. to invent or imagine something

B Complete each sentence with the correct word or phrase from Exercise A. Be sure to use the correct form of the words.

1. Who _____ the idea for that TV commercial?

2. I want to buy my own house soon, but _____, I am living with my grandparents.

3. During the earthquake, many of the buildings began to _____.

4. The river became _____ after the heavy rain.

5. My washing machine is broken, so I have to go to the _____.

6. The _____ promised to paint the rooms before we move into the apartment.

SKILL
FOR
SUCCESS

Recognizing Commonly Confused Words
Some words in English are frequently confused because their pronunciation or spelling is the same or similar. Study the words in the list.

Word	Meaning/Use	Example
here	in this place	The book you want is right **here**.
hear	to perceive sounds with the ear	Please turn up the TV. I can't **hear** it.
it's	(contraction of *it is*)	**It's** small and red with tight steps.
its	(possessive adjective)	The tree has lost **its** leaves.
loose	not attached firmly; not tight-fitting	Her pants are **loose**.
lose	to misplace; to have less of something than you had before	We began to **lose** business after the storm.
quiet	without noise	At night, the house is dark and **quiet**.
quite	very	The new house is **quite** small.
then	at that time; next	I knew **then** I had to have a house.
than	(used with comparisons)	I would rather have coffee **than** tea.

there	in or at a place	You live **there**?
their	(possessive adjective)	They were holding **their** breath.
they're	(contraction of *they are*)	But **they're** ordinary hallway stairs.

two	the number 2	It had been robbed **two** days before.
too	also; more than enough	Be careful not to make **too** much noise.
to	(first word of an infinitive or a preposition)	The family moved **to** Mango Street.

C Complete each sentence with the correct word from the list.

1. We have _____ bathrooms in our new house.

2. Hurry up. _____ already three o'clock. I don't want _____ be late.

3. I'm trying to _____ weight before the summer.

4. The meeting is at the library. I'll meet you _____ at 5:00 P.M.

5. The Lees are having a lot of problems with _____ new computer.

6. The company increased _____ profits last year.

7. This house is _____ expensive. I can't afford to buy it.

8. I had dinner, and _____ I watched TV.

Talk It Over

Discuss these questions in small groups.

1. Why do you think owning a house was so important to Esperanza and her family? Is owning your own house an important goal for you? Why or why not?

2. At the end of the story, Esperanza said, "I knew then I had to have a house. A real house. One I could point to. But this isn't it. The house on Mango Street isn't it. For the time being, Mama says. Temporary, says Papa. But I know how those things go." What do you think she meant by this?

3. Esperanza and her family dreamed of owning their own house. Their dream came partially true. They owned the house on Mango Street, but it wasn't the house of their dreams. Have you ever had a dream that came partially true? How did you feel about it?

My House

Before You Read

A Discuss these questions with a partner.

1. Where were you born? What is your hometown like?
2. What is the best thing you remember about your childhood home?
3. What do you think makes a house a home?

B Learn the meanings of the following words before you read the essay.

stunned (1)	sturdy (2)	novels (3)
strong-willed (1)	absurd (3)	refuge (4)
dissuade (1)	insignificant (3)	

Esperanza felt that her house on Mango Street was like a prison. Now read an essay in which a teenager describes his feelings for the house he is about to leave.

My House

by Daniel Lourie

1   My mother moved a lot when she was growing up. Her family never stayed in any one place more than a year or so because my grandfather was in the army. She hated those years of moving all the time, having to adjust to new schools and make new friends every year. That's why I thought she was joking when she sprang the idea of moving on me. But for once in her life she wasn't joking. This time she was completely serious, and I was stunned. My mother has decided that this house is too big for just the two of us and that an apartment in the city would suit our needs

much better. She is very strong-willed, and when she makes up her mind to do something, it's impossible to dissuade her. Personally, I think she's lost her mind. I guess I can understand why she would want to move, but what about me and what this house means to me?

2   I suppose if you looked at my house, you might think it was just a typical suburban colonial[1], housing just another typical Elkington family. But let me assure you: This sturdy house that has been my home for ten years is anything but typical. My father, my mother, and I moved into this house when I was three years old. I can still remember that first day in our new house like it was yesterday. The first thing I noticed was the enormous front yard. To me it seemed like an ocean of grass—I couldn't wait to dive in. The backyard was full of trees, the gnarled[2] and scary kind that talk at night when the wind blows. But as time went by, I grew to like the trees and the shadows they cast in my room. My father and I built a small tree house in one of the bigger trees. It's still a place I like to go to remember my father and all the wonderful times we had before he died.

3   This house is special—maybe only to me—but special nevertheless. The idea of living in any other house seems absurd. Opening any other front door, looking out any other windows just wouldn't feel like

home. It's the little, seemingly insignificant things, that make this house so special to me: the ice-cold tile floors that make me shiver on midnight snack runs; the paint that creeps away from the molding revealing a rainbow of colors that had peeled, been forgotten, then painted over; the smell of my father's pipe that still lingers in the walls; the towering built-in bookcases that hold my mother's personal library of romance novels and "get-rich-quick" books; the view out my bedroom window.

4   It's not true that we can simply move and make another house our home. This house has been my refuge, my castle, for years. It holds too many important memories, memories that would be lost if we gave it up. A home is more than a dwelling we live in; it takes time to make a house a home.   ■

---

1 colonial – a style of house similar to those popular during the time the United States was a colony of Great Britain

2 gnarled – rough and twisted

After You Read

Comprehension Check

A Read these statements. If a statement is true according to the article, write *T* on the line. If it is false, write *F*.

_____ 1. Daniel's mother didn't like adjusting to new schools every year.

_____ 2. Daniel is excited to move to a new house in the city.

_____ 3. Daniel's mother can't decide if she wants to move to the city or stay in the suburbs.

_____ 4. Daniel's father smoked a pipe.

_____ 5. Daniel's mother rarely jokes.

_____ 6. Daniel's mother likes to read romance novels and "get-rich-quick" books.

_____ 7. Daniel still likes to go to the tree house he built with his father.

_____ 8. As Daniel grew older, he didn't care much about the house he grew up in.

SKILL FOR SUCCESS

Understanding Tone

An author's **tone** is his or her attitude toward a subject. Tone is expressed through the words and details the author chooses to use. Just as a person's speaking voice can express a range of different feelings, an author's writing voice can express many different emotions.

To understand the tone of a passage, think about the author's choice of words. Ask yourself this question: "What emotions do the words express?" Are they hopeful, pessimistic, serious, bitter, fearful, happy, angry, or enthusiastic? The *way* an author says something is often as important as *what* he or she says. Understanding the tone of a reading is an important part of reading comprehension.

B Circle the correct answer.

1. What word best describes the tone of the first paragraph?
   a. joyful
   b. surprised
   c. excited

2. In paragraphs 2 and 3, Daniel describes memories from his childhood home. What emotion best describes his memories?
   a. objective
   b. scornful
   c. sentimental

3. In the final paragraph, Daniel writes about his feelings about what makes a house a home. What word best describes the tone of the paragraph?
   a. humorous
   b. thoughtful
   c. confused

4. Reread paragraph 5 of *The House on Mango Street* (page 67). What is the tone of that paragraph?
   a. disappointed
   b. approving
   c. fearful

5. Reread paragraph 6 of *The House on Mango Street*. What is the tone of that paragraph?
   a. forgiving
   b. embarrassed
   c. admiring

Vocabulary Practice

A Match each word with the correct definition.

Word	Definition
_____ **1.** stunned	**a.** to convince someone not to do something
_____ **2.** strong-willed	**b.** a safe place that gives protection from danger
_____ **3.** dissuade	
_____ **4.** sturdy	**c.** determined to do what you want
_____ **5.** absurd	**d.** unimportant
_____ **6.** insignificant	**e.** physically strong and solid
_____ **7.** refuge	**f.** ridiculous
_____ **8.** novel	**g.** a long printed story about imaginary characters and events
	h. very surprised about something

B Ask and answer these questions with a partner.

1. Who is the most <u>strong-willed</u> person you know?
2. Do you think of your home as a <u>refuge</u>? Why or why not?
3. Do you like to read <u>novels</u>? What is your favorite novel?
4. Once you make up your mind about something, is it easy for someone to <u>dissuade</u> you?
5. When is the last time you were <u>stunned</u> by something that happened in the news?
6. Do you think <u>insignificant</u> things are worth arguing about? Why or why not?
7. Are there any rules at your job or school that you think are <u>absurd</u>? If so, why?
8. If you wanted to build a very <u>sturdy</u> house, what building materials would you use?

SKILL FOR SUCCESS

Learning Antonyms

A word that means the opposite of another word is called an **antonym**. For example, the antonym of *absurd* is *reasonable*. Learning antonyms can increase your vocabulary.

C Read the passage. Find an antonym for each word in the chart that follows the passage. Write the antonyms in the chart.

For eleven months of every year, we live in our modern townhouse in Chicago. But every August my parents, my sister, and I drive to Westport, Massachusetts, to spend a month in the cottage my grandparents built more than fifty years ago. It's just a tiny little cottage, but it's right on the beach, and we adore it. It has only two bedrooms, so it is not very spacious, but it is perfect for the size of our family. After months of living in a busy city, we look forward to our time in a quiet, peaceful place. The best part is that we can walk out the front door and spend the day on our private beach. We can fish, swim, kayak, build sand castles, and do many other things. Even on rainy days, we find plenty of things to do. We read and play cards, or sometimes we go shopping. The cottage isn't heated, so we can only go there in the summer, but I can't imagine anyplace better to go at that time of year. My mother grew from childhood to adulthood in that house, and my sister and I will, too. Three generations of us have loved that tiny cottage, and we each have many wonderful memories of our times there. I hope that when I have children, they will grow up there and love it as much as I do.

Word	Antonym
1. old-fashioned	*modern*
2. cramped	
3. noisy	
4. public	
5. few	
6. awful	

Discuss these questions as a class.

1. How does Daniel Lourie feel about the house he grew up in? What kinds of memories does he describe?
2. What are the differences between the feelings Esperanza (*The House on Mango Street*, page 67) and Daniel have about the houses they grew up in?
3. How do you feel about the place where you grew up? Describe your memories and feelings about that place.

What is important to you in a place to live? Look at the items and circle your answers. Discuss your answers with your classmates.

1 = not important   **2** = somewhat important   **3** = very important

1. Type of building (house, apartment building, etc.) **1**   **2**   **3**
2. Size   **1**   **2**   **3**
3. Yard   **1**   **2**   **3**
4. Friendly neighbors   **1**   **2**   **3**
5. Neighborhood   **1**   **2**   **3**
6. Surroundings (near mountains, beaches, etc.)   **1**   **2**   **3**
7. Near cultural activities (museums, theaters, etc.) **1**   **2**   **3**
8. Near public transportation   **1**   **2**   **3**
9. Other: _____   **1**   **2**   **3**

Birth Order: What It Means for Your Kids . . . and You

Many psychologists believe that birth order (your position in the family, such as eldest or youngest child) is an important factor in shaping your personality. Some even feel that people with the same birth order have more in common with each other than they do with their own siblings.

Before You Read

A Discuss these questions with a partner.

1. How many brothers and sisters do you have? What is your birth order in your family?
2. Is your personality similar to your siblings' personalities? If so, how? If not, how is your personality different?

✓ Using Background Knowledge

B Form three groups with your classmates:

- Group 1: People who are the eldest (or only) child in their family

- Group 2: People who are middle children in their family

- Group 3: People who are the youngest child in their family

With your group, make a list of three or four personality traits that the members of your group have in common, for example, *rebellious, sociable, easygoing*. Write the personality traits in the chart. Choose one member from each group to write the list on the board. Discuss the similarities and differences among the groups.

Eldest Children	Middle Children	Youngest Children
1.	1.	1.
2.	2.	2.
3.	3.	3.
4.	4.	4.

C Learn the meanings of the following words before you read the article.

strive (2)   easygoing (6)   conventional (9)

intense (4)   diplomatic (6)   rebellious (9)

conscientious (4)   sociable (7)   peers (11)

Birth Order: What It Means for Your Kids . . . and You

by Janet Strassman Perlmutter

1 People often wonder how brothers and sisters growing up in the same house and being raised in the same way could turn out to be so different. Many experts believe that what causes such differences among siblings is their place in the family, or their birth order.

2 The idea that being the eldest, middle, or youngest child comes with some typical personality traits has been around since the 1920s, when Austrian psychologist Alfred Adler began stressing the importance of birth order on personality and character. Adler believed that humans have a strong need to be accepted and valued and that family is the first social group in which we strive for this sense of belonging. Adler's theory, and that of several birth-order experts since, is basically this: Children in every family each strive for their parents' love, attention, and resources. The bigger the family, the harder it is to do this. And depending on a child's birth order, he or she responds differently.

Typical Traits

3 Many studies have been conducted comparing the personalities of eldest, middle, and youngest children. Of course, not everyone fits neatly into one category, but generally speaking many share the following characteristics.

1. The Eldest Child

4   Firstborn children have all their parents' attention and resources for a while. Birth-order expert Jack Agati offers the example of the well-organized photo albums parents keep of their first child, documenting every important moment in his or her early life. Firstborns learn that all it takes to gain their parents' approval is to follow their wishes. Eldest children often maintain this approach throughout their lives, gaining status by working hard and not causing problems. Simply put, the firstborn is a good kid who wants to do the right thing, sometimes to the point of being a perfectionist. Firstborns also tend to be emotionally intense and ambitious. They are usually conscientious and often become strong, confident leaders.

5   But things change for the firstborn when other children are born. First children experience being "dethroned[1]" when younger siblings are born. Some psychologists believe this is the defining factor in an eldest child's life. Once eldest children lose their status of being the only child, they work hard to get it back. They usually do this by supporting their parents or other authorities.

2. Middle Children

6   Latter-born children get less attention from their parents. What photo album? As a result, younger children, especially middle children, need to be more creative in capturing their parents' attention. Middle children deal with their position by being adaptable, and they are usually more flexible than firstborns. Middle children are often "people pleasers" and good negotiators. They tend to be cooperative, easygoing, and diplomatic.

3. The Youngest Child

7   Youngest children may face the same struggle for attention and resources as their older "middle" siblings. Or—particularly if there's a large gap in age—youngest children may enjoy a status similar to firstborns, since their parents have more time to focus on them. Youngest children tend to be funny and entertaining. They are usually very sociable people. Parents may have lower expectations for their youngest child. This in turn can cause youngest children to have lower expectations for themselves.

Differing Views

8   The theory of birth order has been around so long you'd think the experts would have an answer by now. In fact, they have lots of different answers and lots of opinions. Some of them are similar, but others are very different.

9   Psychologist Frank Sulloway is one of the leading birth-order experts today. His book *Born to Rebel* examines siblings' competition for their parents' favor. "Siblings are competing for all the goodies," Sulloway observes, listing these as "parental investment, love, affection, and other family resources." Depending on their birth order, children use different strategies to "maximize access to those resources." Firstborns get rewarded for "being helpful and responsible," Sulloway says. They are more conventional because they identify with parents and authority. Firstborns tend to support the status quo[2]. Younger children use different strategies. They are more open to new experiences and willing to take risks. Latter-borns are more likely to be unconventional and rebellious.

10   Sociologist Dalton Conley, author of the book *The Pecking Order*, takes a much

---

[1] **dethroned** – no longer in a powerful or important position

[2] **the status quo** – the way things are at a particular time

different approach. Conley believes that other factors affect personality as much as or more than birth order. Some examples of these are family size, major events like divorce or the death of a parent, and the family's economic situation. As Conley sees it, the success rate of firstborn children has to do with the amount of money and attention that parents can offer a firstborn. As more kids enter the picture, those resources have to be divided. "Firsts and lasts each get some time as an 'only,'" Conley says, noting that this is economically most advantageous. Middle children often get less attention and fewer of the family resources.

11 And then there's Judith Rich Harris, author of *The Nurture Assumption: Why Children Turn Out the Way They Do*. She argues that birth order cannot account for personality differences among siblings, because peers outside the family are the biggest influence on children's personalities—not family relationships. Citing numerous studies, Harris makes a thought-provoking claim: Kids don't act the same or play the same roles outside of their families as they do within their families.

12 Birth order remains a controversial topic. Whether or not you subscribe to theories that birth order can affect your child's personality, ultimately, "we all have free will," Agati notes. It's important for both parents and kids to realize that, despite the characteristics often associated with birth order, "you're not locked into any role." ■

After You Read

Comprehension Check

A Circle the correct answer.

1. According to most birth-order theorists, _____.
   a. bigger families are better than smaller families
   b. a person's personality is not influenced by his or her birth order
   c. eldest, middle, and youngest children from different families share similar characteristics
   d. parents often have very high expectations for their youngest child

2. Why does Jack Agati use the example of the well-organized photo albums?
   a. to show that many parents focus a lot of attention on their first child
   b. to explain how creative parents can be
   c. to teach people how to be good parents
   d. to convince parents not to take so many photos of their first child

3. Who first emphasized the importance of birth order on personality?
   a. Frank Sulloway
   b. Dalton Conley
   c. Jack Agati
   d. Alfred Adler

4. Who believes that birth order cannot account for personality differences among siblings?
   a. Judith Rich Harris
   b. Alfred Adler
   c. Frank Sulloway
   d. Dalton Conley

5. Studies show that middle children _____.
   a. often become strong, confident leaders
   b. are usually more flexible than eldest children
   c. have low expectations for themselves
   d. are poor negotiators

6. According to the article, parental focus _____.
   a. usually increases with second and third children
   b. is often the strongest with first children
   c. is usually the same for all children
   d. is always the strongest with youngest children

7. Dalton Conley uses family size, divorce or the death of a parent, and the family's economic situation as examples of _____.
   a. factors that affect personality as much as or more than birth order
   b. insignificant factors in a child's personality development
   c. the effects of birth order
   d. none of the above

✓ **Paraphrasing**

B Reread the descriptions of eldest children, middle children, and youngest children on page 80 and paraphrase them. Remember: Your paraphrase should express the main idea of the original description as clearly and simply as possible.

1. Eldest children

   _____
   _____
   _____

2. Middle children

   _____
   _____
   _____

3. Youngest children

   _____
   _____
   _____

Using Graphic Organizers: Charts

Graphic organizers are a visual representation of information. They help you understand, organize, and remember information from a reading. **Charts** are one kind of graphic organizer.

C The article describes the theories of three birth-order experts. Complete the chart with information from the article.

Famous youngest Hollywood celebrity children include Cameron Diaz, Jim Carrey, Drew Carey, Whoopi Goldberg, Eddie Murphy, and Billy Crystal.

Name	Book	Theory
1. Frank Sulloway		
2. Dalton Conley		
3. Judith Rich Harris		

Vocabulary Practice

A Circle the correct answer.

1. A <u>conventional</u> person is more likely to _____.
   a. break the rules of society   b. follow the customs of society

2. Which is characteristic of a <u>conscientious</u> student?
   a. She always does her homework.   b. She rarely does her homework.

3. A <u>rebellious</u> child is _____.
   a. easy to control   b. difficult to control

4. Most <u>sociable</u> people _____.
   a. enjoy going to parties   b. avoid going to parties

5. People who <u>strive</u> for perfection in their work _____.
   a. try their hardest   b. don't try very hard

6. A <u>diplomatic</u> person will try to _____.
   a. solve problems between   b. cause problems
      two people   between his friends

7. An <u>intense</u> person probably _____.
   a. has strong opinions   b. doesn't have strong feelings
      about many things   or opinions

8. An <u>easygoing</u> person is _____ worried or annoyed.
   a. often   b. rarely

9. Who are your <u>peers</u>?
   a. your classmates   b. your grandparents

✓ **Learning Synonyms and Antonyms**

B For each pair of words, circle *S* if they are synonyms or *A* if they are antonyms.

1. conventional	traditional	(S)	A
2. peers	colleagues	S	A
3. easygoing	intense	S	A
4. strive	try hard	S	A
5. conscientious	careful	S	A
6. rebellious	conforming	S	A
7. sociable	outgoing	S	A
8. conscientious	careless	S	A
9. diplomatic	tactful	S	A

Talk It Over

Discuss these questions as a class.

1. Do you think birth order is an important factor in shaping personality? Why or why not?
2. Do you think your own personality was shaped by your position in your family? If so, in what ways?
3. What other factors do you think influenced your personality, such as your gender, culture, and so on?

Reading a Short Story

Richard Shelton is the author of twelve books of poetry. He has also written scripts for several short films, nonfiction books, and short stories, such as "The Stones." In this story, Shelton brings stones to life, describing them as if they were people.

Read "The Stones." Then do the activities that follow the story.

The Stones

by Richard Shelton

I love to go out on summer nights and watch the stones grow. I think they grow better here in the desert, where it is warm and dry, than almost anywhere else. Or perhaps it is only that the young ones are more active here.

Young stones tend to move about more than their elders think is good for them. Most young stones have a secret desire which their parents had before them but have forgotten a long time ago. And because this desire involves water, it is never mentioned. The older stones disapprove of water. They say, "Water is a gadfly[1] who never stays in one place long enough to learn anything." But the young stones try to work themselves into a position, slowly and without their elders noticing it, so a big stream of water during a summer storm might catch them and unknowingly push them along over a slope[2] or down an arroyo[3]. In spite of the danger this involves, they want to travel and see something of the world and settle in a new place, far from home, where they can raise their own families away from the control of their parents.

And although family ties are very strong among stones, many of the more daring young ones have succeeded, and they carry

scars to prove to their children that they once went on a journey and traveled perhaps fifteen feet, an incredible distance. As they grow older, they stop bragging about those secret adventures.

It is true that old stones get to be very conservative. They consider all movement either dangerous or sinful. They remain comfortable where they are and often get fat. Fatness, as a matter of fact, is a mark of distinction.

And on summer nights, after the young stones are asleep, the elders turn to a serious and frightening subject—the moon, which is always spoken of in whispers. "See how it glows and whips across the sky, always changing its shape," one says. And another says, "Feel how it pulls at us, urging us to follow." And a third whispers, "It is a stone gone mad[4]."

---

[1] **gadfly** – something annoying

[2] **slope** – a piece of land that is higher at one end than the other

[3] **arroyo** – a narrow, deep piece of land that fills with water when it rains

[4] **mad** – crazy

A Discuss these questions in small groups.

1. Did you like this story? Why or why not?
2. Shelton writes, "Most young stones have a secret desire which their parents had before them but have forgotten a long time ago." Do you have a secret desire? What is it?
3. Why do the young stones want to settle in a new place? Do you want to settle in a new place? Why or why not?
4. What do the old stones think about water? What do you think water represents in the story?
5. In what ways do the stones change as they get older? Do you think people change in similar ways?
6. What is a mark of distinction for the old stones? What are some marks of distinction for older people?
7. What do you think of when you look at the moon? Why do the old stones believe that the moon is a stone that has gone crazy?

SKILL FOR SUCCESS

Understanding Figurative Language

Figurative language refers to words or phrases used in a different way from the usual one to help create a picture in your mind. Authors often use figurative language to make their writing more vivid. *Similes*, *metaphors*, and *personification* are some examples of figurative language. Study the definitions and examples in the chart that follows.

B Which of the following types of figurative language did Richard Shelton use in "The Stones"?

	Definition	Example
Simile	An expression in which two things are compared by using the words *like* or *as*	*He was so scared that his face turned as white as snow.*
Metaphor	A way of describing something by comparing it to something else that has similar qualities, without using the words *like* or *as*	*I cried a river of tears.*
Personification	Representation of inanimate objects or abstract ideas as living beings	*Justice is blind.*

C Read the following sentences that use figurative language. Write *S* if the sentence is an example of a simile, write *M* if it is a metaphor, and write *P* if it shows personification.

_____S_____ 1. My thoughts are as deep as the deepest ocean.

_____ 2. Happiness is a flower that blossoms in my heart.

_____ 3. All the world's a stage, and all the men and women merely players. —William Shakespeare

_____ 4. She's a wild horse of a woman. —Sandra Cisneros

_____ 5. The stars danced lightly across the sky.

_____ 6. My love is like a red, red rose. —Robert Burns

_____ 7. She flew like a bird.

_____ 8. The bad news was like a knife in her heart.

_____ 9. His words were music to my ears.

_____ 10. The moon looked down and smiled at me.

Discussion

Discuss these questions in a small group.

1. What does the expression "Home is where the heart is" mean to you? What about this expression: "A house is not a home"?
2. Primo Levi (1919–1987) was an Italian chemist and author. He said, "I live in my house as I live inside my skin: I know more beautiful, more ample, more sturdy, and more picturesque skins; but it would seem to me unnatural to exchange them for mine." Do you feel like that about your house?
3. Does birth order play an important role in your society? Are firstborn children given any special treatment? What about youngest children?

Just For Fun

Look at the drawings and try to remember as much about them as you can. Then cover the drawings and list all the differences between the two pictures that you can remember.

A

B

_____   _____

_____   _____

_____   _____

_____   _____

The Role of Birth Order in History
Thinking back to your reading in Chapter 3, do you agree that younger siblings are generally more adventurous than firstborn children? If so, do you think perhaps younger siblings have always, throughout history, been more flexible and tolerant of new ideas? Can you think of an example?

A Study these words. Then watch the video.

achievement	hotbed	sibling rivalry
championing	racial integration	Supreme Court Justices
dogged	rebel	

B Watch the video again. Then complete these sentences with information from the video.

1. Frank Sulloway claims that birth order affects _____
   _____.

2. Sulloway describes later-born children as _____
   _____.

3. Some examples Sulloway gives of adventurous younger siblings are
   _____
   _____.

4. Sulloway examines historical periods and concludes that younger siblings are more likely to _____
   _____.

5. Sulloway explains that firstborns automatically get the love and attention of their parents, while younger siblings must come up with
   _____
   _____.

C Discuss this question with a partner or in a small group.

Think of a historical figure who advanced new ideas or fought for change. Use the Internet to find out if this person was a firstborn child or a younger sibling. Does your example support Sulloway's argument? Compare your results with the class.

Reader's Journal   Think about the topics and ideas you have read about and discussed in this unit. Pick a topic from the following list, choose one of the discussion questions in the unit, or write about an idea of your own. Write about it for ten to twenty minutes.

- a description of your house
- your feelings about the place you grew up in
- your place in your family
- what "home" means to you

Vocabulary Self-Test

Complete each sentence with the correct word or phrase.

A for the time being   refuge   sturdy
    insignificant   stunned   swollen
    novels

1. I was _____ when I heard that I had won first prize. My parents were just as surprised.

2. I like to read _____ about people my own age who go on adventures.

3. I don't think I'll live here forever, but _____ I'll stay in this apartment.

4. Most of the buildings in this area are very _____, so they weren't damaged during the storm.

5. Don't worry about such a small and _____ amount of money.

6. My room is my _____. I go there when I need to feel safe and secure.

7. Your eyes look _____. Have you been crying?

B crumble   intense   peers
    dissuade   landlord   strong-willed
    dream up   Laundromat

1. When the washing machine in my apartment broke, the _____ gave me money to go to a(n) _____.

2. He's a very _____ young man. Once he makes up his mind to do something, no one can stop him.

3. The old wall is starting to _____.

4. He is shy around adults, but he gets along well with his
   _____.

5. How did you ever _____ that ridiculous story? I don't
   believe any of it.

6. I tried to _____ her from leaving the party so early, but
   she left anyway.

7. My sister is the only _____ one in our family. The rest of
   us are quite easygoing.

C absurd   diplomatic   sociable
   conscientious   easygoing   strive
   conventional   rebellious

1. Jason is the most _____ person I know. He never
   worries about anything.

2. My grandmother is very _____. She would never think
   of doing anything that goes against the traditions of our culture.

3. He puts a lot of effort into his schoolwork. I think he's one of the
   most _____ students in the class.

4. She is always getting in trouble because of her _____
   nature. She hates to follow the rules.

5. You should try to go out and be more _____. You spend
   too much time alone in the library.

6. I always _____ to do my best.

7. He was able to negotiate the peace treaty because of his
   _____ skills.

8. You look _____ in that big hat. Please take it off.

WINNING AND LOSING

Competition is a big part of sports and many other aspects of life. Most of us would rather win than lose, but the reality is that we all lose sometimes. Learning how to put both winning and losing into perspective is something that comes with experience.

Florence Griffith-Joyner winning the 100-meter race at the 1988 Olympics in Seoul

Points to Ponder

Think about these questions and discuss them in a small group.

1. What does it mean to be a winner in your culture? What are the outward signs of success?
2. Is the concept of being a team player important in your culture? In what areas other than sports, such as school and business, is it important?
3. How important is winning to you personally? Are you someone who always has to win?

U N I T 4

CHAPTER 1

Athletes as Role Models

Before You Read

A Discuss these questions with a partner.

1. A role model is a person that other people admire and whose behavior they try to copy. Do you have a role model? Who?
2. Do you think famous athletes should act as role models? What about movie stars? Politicians? Religious leaders?
3. In your native country, are athletes celebrities? Do they serve as role models?

✓ **Previewing and Predicting**

B Read the title and the five headings in bold print. Then skim the article by reading the first and last paragraphs and the first sentence of all the other paragraphs. Use the information to make predictions about the kinds of things the author might discuss in the article.

_____

_____

_____

_____

_____

C Learn the meanings of the following words and phrases before you read the article.

perseverance (3)	mentors (3)	get caught up in (7)
keep their cool (3)	flaws (4)	cheering (7)
high-profile (3)	take in stride (7)	distracted (9)

Athletes as Role Models

by Sheila Globus

1 Everyone loves sports stars. They look great, they appear on television, and like rock stars, they perform with the entire world watching. No wonder we make heroes out of our favorites. Great athletes teach us more than how to swing a bat or block a pass. In the face of seemingly impossible challenges, they teach us that success—whether on the basketball court or in the classroom—takes dedication, confidence, and a lot of hard work.

Sports Stars Are People, Too

2 Athletes are seen as heroes because they can do things that most of us can't do. Some can hit fastballs coming at them at nearly 100 miles an hour. Others can jump and hang in the air or throw a ball over a net. They get paid millions of dollars for their efforts, and their names and faces appear on everything from running shoes to billboards. Their words are repeated and broadcast around the world.

3 Athletes who are champions also show personal qualities such as perseverance, dedication, generosity, and the ability to keep their cool under pressure. Many show those same qualities off the playing field, too. Stories about superstar athletes teach us about working hard and believing in yourself and about being passionate about what we do. Although it's usually bad behavior that gets an athlete on the six o'clock news, many high-profile players work hard to be positive role models to children. They raise money for charities and act as mentors, talking to student groups and volunteering their time to programs that help kids stay off drugs and stay in school.

4 Still, even the greatest champions have flaws. Just because an athlete has the perfect golf swing doesn't mean he or she is the perfect parent, friend, or spokesperson. Even rich, famous, and successful people get sick and face the same problems other people do. They also make mistakes. Separating an athlete's professional and personal life can be tough. When a sports star gets in trouble with the law, or does something wrong in his or her private life, fans often feel disappointed. Before he died, baseball great Mickey Mantle, who had serious alcohol problems, told young ball players and the fans who idolized and admired him to "play like me; don't be like me."

Against All Odds

5 Some sports heroes have overcome many obstacles to rise to the top of their sport. In 1947, for example, baseball player Jackie Robinson of the Brooklyn Dodgers overcame racism to become the first African American to play in the modern major leagues. Former Olympian Wilma Rudolph had to overcome several serious illnesses. She survived pneumonia and scarlet fever as a child. She then contracted polio, which left her with a bad leg that some people said would prevent her even from walking. Although she wore a leg brace from the time she was 5 until she was 11, Rudolph still managed to play basketball and go out for track[1] when she was 13. While still a high school

---

[1] **track** – the sport of running races

sophomore, she competed in the 1956 Olympic Games. These days, Rudolph is remembered for her inspirational determination to overcome her physical challenges, and for her courage in rising above segregation and racism.

6 Few athletes have achieved as many victories as cyclist Lance Armstrong. But he had to overcome many obstacles in order to achieve those victories. Lance rose to the top of the cycling world by the time he was 25. In 1996, he was ranked number one. Then he was diagnosed with cancer. Doctors predicted that he had little chance of recovery. However, Lance was determined to fight the cancer, and amazingly, his health recovered. Within a year of medical treatments, he was able to begin training again. Lance has won many races, including the very difficult Tour de France an amazing seven times in a row, and many honors, including *Sports Illustrated*'s "Sportsman of the Year" and the Associated Press's "Male Athlete of the Year." Through his impressive cycling victories and his amazing recovery from illness, Lance Armstrong stands out as an example of skill, determination, and courage.

Cyclist Lance Armstrong has overcome many obstacles.

Keeping Things in Perspective

7 Courage and determination aren't the only lessons we can learn from successful athletes. Some of the greatest sports figures, past and present, are those who can look at their athletic achievements and take them in stride. You have to love a sport to do it and to do it well. But you also have to know how not to get caught up in the glory, especially when the crowds are cheering for somebody else.

8 Hardworking and highly motivated athletes understand that there is more to sports than winning. Being the top scorer or having the best batting average or the fastest time is less important than just giving it your best shot, whatever the outcome. Champion distance runner Joan Benoit Samuelson says it best: "Winning is neither everything nor the only thing. It is one of many things."

The Power of Positive Thinking

9 Athletes like Michael Jordan can sink a foul shot in front of thousands of people waving their arms and shouting without getting distracted. Did you ever wonder how they do it? Great athletes use the power of positive thinking. They can focus their total concentration on the task at hand. They also arrive at the field, rink, or pool feeling like a winner. They visualize winning and tackle each game or event with spirit and determination. Overconfident? Not really. How often does the team rated the underdog[2] win the game?

Being Your Best

10 To rise to the top of any profession or sport takes countless hours of practice to fine-tune the skills needed to accomplish

---

[2] **underdog** – the person or team that is not expected to win

your goals. But star athletes learn from their mistakes as well as from their successes. They have what it takes to be a winner. Remember that qualities like fairness, sportsmanship, honesty, and determination also can be found in everyday people—your teachers, a coach at school, and your parents. ■

After You Read

A Answer these questions.

1. According to the article, what is the most important thing that sports heroes teach us?

   _____

   _____

2. Why are athletes often seen as heroes?

   _____

3. What are some things that high-profile players do to be positive role models to children?

   _____

   _____

4. Why did baseball superstar Mickey Mantle tell his fans, "Play like me; don't be like me"?

   _____

   _____

5. What obstacles did each of the following athletes have to overcome to achieve success?
   a. Jackie Robinson: _____

   _____

   b. Wilma Rudolph: _____

   _____

   c. Lance Armstrong: _____

   _____

6. What do highly motivated top athletes understand about winning?

   _____

   _____

7. What does it take to rise to the top and accomplish your goals?

   _____

   _____

8. According to the article, what qualities does it take to be a winner?

   _____

✓ **Making Inferences**

B Check (✔) the statements you think the author would agree with.

❑ 1. Being the best and winning are the most important aspects of sports.

❑ 2. To be at the top of any profession or sport takes a commitment to practice and hard work.

❑ 3. Great athletes teach us more than just the skill of their sport.

❑ 4. All great champions are perfect.

❑ 5. Underdogs win because they are determined and focused.

❑ 6. You don't have to be a star athlete to be a winner.

❑ 7. It's impossible not to get caught up in the glory when you're a sports star.

❑ 8. Only athletes can be good role models.

SKILL ✓ FOR ✔ SUCCESS

Identifying Supporting Information
You have learned that a paragraph usually has one main idea. Main ideas are supported with **facts, reasons, and examples.** After you identify the main idea, look for information that supports it. Understanding the relationship between the main idea and the supporting sentences will improve your reading comprehension.

C Read these statements. In each group, write *M* in front of the statement that expresses a main idea. Write *S* in front of statements that give supporting information.

1. _____ a. Some can hit fastballs coming at them at nearly 100 miles an hour.

_____ b. Athletes are seen as heroes because they can do things that most of us can't do.

_____ c. Others can jump and hang in the air, or throw a ball over a net.

2. _____ a. In 1947, for example, baseball player Jackie Robinson of the Brooklyn Dodgers overcame racism to become the first African American to play in the modern major leagues.

_____ b. Former Olympian Wilma Rudolph had to overcome several serious illnesses.

_____ c. Some sports heroes have overcome many obstacles to rise to the top of their sport.

3. _____ a. Although it's usually bad behavior that gets an athlete on the six o'clock news, many high-profile players work hard to be positive role models to children.

   _____ b. Athletes who are champions also show important personal qualities both on and off the playing field.

   _____ c. They raise money for charities and act as mentors, talking to student groups and volunteering their time to programs that help kids stay off drugs and stay in school.

4. _____ a. Hardworking and highly motivated athletes understand that there is more to sports than winning.

   _____ b. Being the top scorer or having the best batting average or the fastest time is less important than just giving it your best shot, whatever the outcome.

   _____ c. Champion distance runner Joan Benoit Samuelson says it best: "Winning is neither everything nor the only thing. It is one of many things."

5. _____ a. Athletes like Michael Jordan can sink a foul shot in front of thousands of people waving their arms and shouting without getting distracted.

   _____ b. They visualize winning and tackle each game or event with spirit and determination.

   _____ c. Great athletes use the power of positive thinking.

Vocabulary Practice

A Complete each sentence with the correct word or phrase. Be sure to use the correct form of the words.

cheer	get caught up in	mentor
distracted	high-profile	perseverance
flaw	keep their cool	take it in stride

1. Everyone has heard of Jason McCoy. He was already a _____ athlete when he decided to go into politics.

2. He made a lot of mistakes in the game because he was thinking about something else and got _____.

3. The politician got a lot of criticism, but he _____.

4. She _____ the glory of being a superstar and forgot all about her friends.

5. My supervisor at work is my _____. She taught me everything I know about how to be a good nurse.

6. He's good at golf, not because he's a gifted athlete, but because he has _____ and practices every chance he gets.

7. No one is perfect all the time. Everyone has _____.

8. I jumped up and _____ when my team won the basketball game.

9. I don't know how the people who work here manage to _____ in such a hectic office.

B Ask and answer these questions with a partner.

1. Did you ever get caught up in an argument that didn't really concern you?
2. Do you get distracted if people are talking while you are reading?
3. What high-profile athlete do you admire?
4. Do you have a mentor? Who?
5. If you could change one flaw in your personality, what would it be?
6. Do you think perseverance is an important part of being good at a sport? Why?
7. When do you cheer for people besides at sports events?
8. Do you find it hard to keep your cool when you are angry?
9. What kinds of things do you have trouble taking in stride?

SKILL FOR SUCCESS ✓ **Understanding Word Parts: The Suffixes -ance and -ence**
In this chapter, you learned the meaning of the word *perseverance*. It is formed by adding the **suffix** -*ance* to the verb *persevere*. The suffixes -*ance* and -*ence* are used to make nouns from adjectives and verbs.

C Add the suffix -*ance* or -*ence* to each word to make a noun. Use your dictionary for help with spelling. Then write a sentence using each word.

1. resist: _____ *resistance* _____

   _____

2. absent: _____

   _____

3. exist: _____

   _____

4. perform: _____

_____

5. accept: _____

_____

6. prefer: _____

_____

7. insure: _____

_____

Discuss these questions as a class.

1. Many people expect athletes to lead perfect lives. Do you think it's fair to expect athletes to live up to such high standards? Why or why not?
2. If you hear that an athlete has done something illegal or immoral, are you very disappointed? Do you judge him or her more harshly than you would someone else? Why or why not?
3. What personal qualities do you think make someone a good role model?
4. Do you agree or disagree with Joan Benoit Samuelson's opinion that "Winning is neither everything nor the only thing. It is one of many things"?
5. Do you agree or disagree with basketball star Charles Barkley's statement, "I am not a role model . . . parents should be role models"?

Olympic Marathons, Then and Now

The best-known athletic competition in the world is the Olympics. The Olympics bring together athletes from every corner of the world to compete for the chance to be the best.

Before You Read

A Discuss these questions in a small group.

1. Have you ever watched or participated in a marathon?
2. Why do you think so many people like to torture themselves by running for more than 26 miles without stopping?
3. Marathoners train very hard before a race. Do you participate in any sport that requires a lot of training? If so, how do you prepare for competitions?

✓ **Reading with a Purpose**

B You are going to read an article about the history of marathons. Write three questions you hope will be answered in the article.

1. _____
2. _____
3. _____

C Learn the meanings of the following words and phrase before you read the article.

spectators (2)   delight (4)   triumph (9)
running neck and neck (3) suspense (6)
exhaustion (4)   collapsed (6)

Olympic Marathons, Then and Now

by Mary Evans Andrews

1 The starter's gun fired into the bright blue sky over Greece. Twenty-five runners took off from the bridge at the town of Marathon. It was 2:00 P.M. on April 10, 1896, and the first marathon race in history had just begun. It was part of the first Olympic Games in modern history. Almost 25 miles away, in the white marble stadium of Athens, 79,000 people waited to cheer the winner. In the royal box seats, King George I of Greece and his two sons waited to award the medals. Almost everyone hoped that a Greek would win the marathon.

2 The Games were nearly over, and no Greek athlete had won a medal. How embarrassing for the country that had begun the ancient Olympics in 776 B.C. For this long race, thousands of spectators lined the uphill road from Marathon to Athens. At the first village, a Frenchman was far in the lead. A mile back came men from Australia, the United States, and Hungary. Not one Greek ran among the leaders.

3 Several minutes later, Spyridon Loues jogged by. Small and thin, Spyro was a 25-year-old shepherd[1] from the hills near Athens. "Faster!" the anxious villagers urged him on. "The foreigners are far ahead!" Spyro had spent the day before the race praying and fasting[2]. "Never mind," he said calmly. "I will overtake them all!" Meanwhile, the French runner was still first, and the Australian was second. The American had fallen down and couldn't continue. As the road climbed toward Athens, Spyro ran smoothly past the Frenchman and for a few kilometers he was running neck and neck with the Australian. Soon, Spyro sailed into first place. He had only seven kilometers to go.

4 A messenger on horseback rode off to alert the crowd in the stadium. A Greek was in the lead! He should win—if he didn't drop from exhaustion. When Spyro was sighted from the stadium, the king's sons ran to the entrance to greet him. They ran with him to the finish—as the crowd roared in delight. Spyro's time was 2 hours, 58 minutes, and 50 seconds.

5 Seven minutes after he had crossed the line, a second runner finished, then a third. Both were Greeks. The stadium went wild. When the medals were awarded, Spyro, as first-place winner, received an olive branch and a silver medal. In those days, gold medals were not awarded. The second-place winner received a bronze medal.

---

[1] **shepherd** – someone whose job it is to take care of sheep

[2] **fast** – to eat very little or nothing for a period of time

6 Nearly 2,400 years before this race, in 490 B.C., a Greek soldier had run the same course[3] from Marathon to Athens. After fighting all day in a battle against the Persians, he was bringing news of the Greek victory. Against incredible odds, the small Greek army had won the battle. All that day, the frightened Athenians waited in suspense. When the soldier finally got to Athens, he said, "Rejoice! We have conquered!" Then he collapsed and died. All modern marathons honor his heroic run.

7 The marathon has been part of every Olympics since the modern games began in 1896. It is usually the last event of the Games. Until 1984, it was an event for men only. There were, of course, female long-distance runners before the 1980s, but they were not allowed to compete in the Olympic Games. But that year in Los Angeles, American runner Joan Benoit Samuelson made history when she won the first women's Olympic marathon. Her time of 2 hours, 24 minutes, 52 seconds remained the fastest women's record until the Sydney Olympics of 2000 when the Japanese runner Naoko Takahashi beat it by 1 minute, 28 seconds. How long will her record of 2 hours, 23 minutes, 14 seconds hold?

8 There are no age limits for Olympic contestants. Juan Zabala, from Argentina, was 20 when he won at Los Angeles in 1932. The oldest champion, Mamo Wolde, from Ethiopia, was 36 when he won at Mexico City in 1968.

9 Like all marathons, each Olympic marathon is different. Weather conditions vary; the course may be hilly or flat. But in all marathons, runners must overcome physical and mental challenges: aching muscles, cramps, thirst, hurt feet, exhaustion, and even boredom. In the end, one important thing remains the same—the feeling of triumph in running the distance. All who finish are winners. Like the ancient Greek messenger, they can say, "Rejoice! We have conquered!" ■

---

[3] **course** – a place in which a race is held or a particular type of sport is played

After You Read

Comprehension Check

A Circle the correct answer.

1. In the first modern marathon, _____.
   a. three Greek men were the fastest runners
   b. a French runner came in first and an Australian was second
   c. not one Greek was among the three fastest runners
   d. a man from the United States won the silver medal

2. According to the article, _____.
   a. all marathons are exactly the same
   b. all marathons are different in some ways
   c. marathons are predictable and easy to win
   d. some marathons are much longer than others

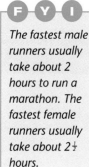

The fastest male runners usually take about 2 hours to run a marathon. The fastest female runners usually take about 2½ hours.

3. Which of the following is NOT true about modern Olympic marathons?
   a. There are no age limits for participants.
   b. The marathon is usually the last event of the Games.
   c. Women are not allowed to participate in Olympic marathon races.
   d. The modern marathon honors the heroic run of a Greek soldier.

4. Why did a Greek soldier run from Marathon to Athens in 490 B.C.?
   a. He was participating in a marathon.
   b. He was running away from the Persian army.
   c. He was bringing news of a Greek victory.
   d. He was running to join the Greek army in Athens.

5. Which is NOT mentioned as a problem for runners in the article?
   a. hunger
   b. thirst
   c. cramps
   d. boredom

SKILL FOR SUCCESS

Scanning for Information

Scanning is a way to read quickly in order to find a specific piece of information in a text. You usually scan to find a name, a date, a time, a place, or a definition. To scan, move your eyes quickly down the page until you find the information you are looking for and then stop reading. It helps to think about how the information you are looking for will be presented. For example, if you want to know *when* something happened, scan for a date. If you want to know *who* did something, scan for a name. Ignore words and information that are not important for your purpose.

B Scan the article for the answer to each question. Work as quickly as possible.

1. When did the first modern marathon race begin?
   April 10, 1896

2. Who won the marathon in the 1896 Olympic Games?
   Spyro / Spyridon

3. How long did it take Spyridon to run the marathon?
   2 hrs, 58 minutes, 50 seconds

4. Who won the first women's Olympic marathon?
   Joan Benoit Samuelson

5. What was her time? 2 hrs, 24 mins, 52 sec.

6. How old was Mamo Wolde when he won the marathon at Mexico City in 1968? 36 yrs old

7. What country was Juan Zabala from? Argentina

Recognizing Sequence

Recognizing the sequence of events (the order in which events happen, also called *time order*) in a reading passage is an important reading skill. As you read, look for clues that give you information about the order of events, such as dates, times, and signal words. Here are some common words that signal time order.

after	last	second
before	later	then
finally	meanwhile	when
first	next	

C Number these events so that they are in the order in which they happened.

_____9___ **a.** The oldest Olympic marathon champion, Mamo Wolde, from Ethiopia, was 36 when he won at Mexico City in 1968.

3___~~8~~___ **b.** At 2:00 P.M. on April 10, 1896, the first Olympic marathon race in history began.

___~~7~~___ **c.** Seven minutes after Spyro had crossed the line, a second runner finished, then a third. Both were Greeks.

_____1___ **d.** In 490 B.C., a Greek soldier ran from Marathon to Athens bringing news of the Greek victory.

4___~~3~~___ **e.** At the first village, a Frenchman was far in the lead. A mile back came men from Australia, the United States, and Hungary.

5___~~4~~___ **f.** Several minutes later, Spyridon Loues jogged by.

___~~10~~___ **g.** American runner Joan Benoit Samuelson made history in 1984 when she won the first women's Olympic marathon.

2___~~5~~___ **h.** Spyro spent the day before the race praying and fasting.

___~~6~~___ **i.** When Spyro crossed the finish line, his time was 2 hours, 58 minutes, and 50 seconds.

___~~11~~___ **j.** In 2000, the Japanese runner Naoko Takahashi beat Samuelson's time by 1 minute, 28 seconds.

___~~8~~___ **k.** Juan Zabala, from Argentina, was 20 when he won at Los Angeles in 1932.

SKILL FOR SUCCESS

Using Graphic Organizers: Making a Timeline

Remember that **graphic organizers** help you organize information.
Timelines are another kind of graphic organizer. Timelines show important
dates and events.

D Make a timeline about the history of marathons. Include the dates and
events you think are important. Find some additional information about
the history of marathons on the Internet or at the library and include it on
the timeline.

from article

| 490 B.C. |

Greek soldier ran from
Marathon to Athens with
news of the Greek victory.

Vocabulary Practice

A Complete each sentence with the correct word or phrase. Be sure to use
the correct form of the words.

~~collapse~~   running neck and neck   suspense
delight   ~~spectator~~   ~~triumph~~
~~exhaustion~~

1. The little boy smiled in __delight__ when he saw the birthday
   cake and presents.

2. The __spectator__ clapped and cheered as the first-place runner
   crossed the finish line.

3. The old man __collapse__ when he had a heart attack.

4. Running the whole marathon was a personal __triumph__ for
   me.

5. The two candidates were __running__ for most of the
   campaign, and the election ended in a tie.

6. The audience watched the final scene of the scary movie in
   __exhaustion__. Suspense

7. She hadn't slept in two days and felt sick from __exhaustion__.

Learning Idioms: Expressions about Competition and Sports
In this chapter, you learned the idiom *running neck and neck*. English speakers use many idioms that have to do with **competition and sports**.

B Match each idiom with the correct definition.

Idiom	Definition
_f_ **1.** be on the ball	**a.** very unusual
_i_ **2.** par for the course	**b.** to be aware of and prepared for all possibilities
_d_ **3.** hit below the belt	**c.** an approximate number
_h_ **4.** throw in the towel	**d.** to attack unfairly
_g_ **5.** be in someone's corner	**e.** rescued or saved from a difficult or unpleasant situation by a welcome interruption
_e_ **6.** saved by the bell	**f.** to be quick to understand and react to things
_c_ **7.** a ballpark figure	**g.** to be on someone's side
_a_ **8.** out in left field	**h.** to give up
_b_ **9.** cover all the bases	**i.** normal, as you would expect

C Complete each sentence with the correct idiom from Exercise B. Be sure to use the correct form of the words.

1. Her argument made no sense. It was completely _out in the left field_.

2. You still have a chance of wining. Don't _throw in the towel_ yet.

3. I don't know exactly how much that car cost, but I can give you _a ballpark figure_.

4. The teacher was just about to call on me to answer a question I wasn't sure of. Luckily, another student yelled out the answer just in time. I was _hit below_ .

5. Even if everyone else disagrees with you, don't worry. I'm _be in someone's corner_, and I'll defend you.

F Y I

The top average speed for Winter Olympic sports is in downhill skiing—65 miles per hour.

6. When you criticized me in front of my family, you were really _hit below the belt_.

7. If you don't get a good night's sleep, you won't feel alert and _be on the ball_ in class tomorrow.

8. Before you make a decision to go ahead with this plan, you should make sure you have _saved by the bell_.

9. My plane was late, but that's _par for the course_ for this airline. They have a reputation for being late.

✓ **Learning Synonyms and Antonyms**

D For each pair of words, circle *S* if they are synonyms or *A* if they are antonyms.

1. exhaustion	fatigue	S	A
2. triumph	failure	S	A
3. delight	displeasure	S	A
4. suspense	anticipation	S	A
5. collapse	fall down	S	A
6. spectator	participant	S	A

Reading Descriptions

Read the information about the Olympic symbols and traditions on page 110. Then, in a small group, discuss the questions that follow the information.

Olympic Symbols and Traditions

The Symbol: The five interlocking rings of the Olympics are one of the most familiar symbols in the world. The symbol of the Olympics, five circles that are linked together, represents good sportsmanship among all peoples. The rings also symbolize five continents—Europe, Asia, Africa, Australia, and the Americas. Each ring is a different color—blue, yellow, black, green, and red. The Olympic flag shows the symbol of the five rings.

The Motto of the Olympics: A *motto* is a phrase or expression used to encourage action. The motto of the Olympics—"Citius, Altius, Fortius"—is Latin and means "faster, higher, braver." The motto was written by Henri Martin Didon, a French educator, in 1895.

The Olympic Creed: A *creed* is a system of beliefs. The Olympic creed is "The most important thing in the Olympic Games is not to win but to take part, just as the most important thing in life is not the triumph but the struggle. The essential thing is not to have conquered but to have fought well."

The Olympic Oath: An *oath* is a pledge or promise. At the opening ceremony of the Olympics, one of the athletes from the host country recites the following oath: "In the name of all competitors, I promise that we will take part in these Olympic Games, respecting and abiding by the rules which govern them, in the true spirit of sportsmanship, for the glory of sport and the honor of our teams." The oath and the creed were both written by Pierre de Coubertin, the founder of the modern Olympics.

The Flame: The flame symbolizes the connection between the original and the modern games. The flame is carried from Olympia, Greece, to the site of the Games by relays of thousands of runners. Planes and ships carry the flame across mountains and water. It continues to burn until the Games are over.

The Opening Ceremony: The opening ceremonies of the Olympic Games are very exciting. They begin with a parade of all the athletes into the stadium. The Greek athletes always go first in honor of the original Olympics. The other countries follow in alphabetical order. The government leader of the host country then announces that the Games have begun. Trumpets play and cannons are fired as the Olympic flag is raised. Hundreds of doves are set free as a symbol of peace. The grand finale is a spectacular show performed by local artists.

1. The five interlocking rings of the Olympics are one of the most familiar symbols in the world. What two things does the symbol represent? Why do you think this symbol is an appropriate representation of the Olympic Games?

2. The Olympic flag shows the symbol of the five rings. Describe your national flag. The 50 stars on the flag of the United States symbolize the 50 states in the union. The 13 stripes represent the original 13 colonies. What does your national flag symbolize?

3. How is the Olympic motto a guide to the participants in the Games? The motto of the French Revolution was "Liberty, Equality, Fraternity." What other mottoes can you think of?

4. According to the Olympic creed, what is the most important thing in the Games? How does this relate to life in general? Do you agree with the message of the Olympic creed? Why or why not?

5. An oath is a pledge or promise. What do the athletes promise to do in the Olympics?

6. What does the Olympic flame symbolize?

7. The opening ceremonies of the Olympic Games are always very impressive. Have you ever seen the ceremonies in person? On television? In your opinion, what makes them so exciting?

Helping Athletes Go for the Gold

Before You Read

A Discuss these questions with a partner.

1. There is a lot more to sports than just physical abilities. Do you think mental skills are important, too? Why or why not?
2. Do you think psychologists can help athletes deal with stress and set goals? Why or why not?

B Learn the meanings of the following words and phrases before you read the article.

potential (3)	stick with it (6)	triggers (12)
consultation (5)	equivalent (8)	tactics (13)
down the road (6)		

As You Read

 Paraphrasing

You are going to read an interview with psychologist Richard Suinn. After you read each of Dr. Suinn's answers, paraphrase what he said in your own words. Write on the lines given in the article.

Helping Athletes Go for the Gold

by Robert Epstein

1   Sports psychologist Richard Suinn, Ph.D., of Colorado State University, is a man familiar with firsts: In 1972, he became the first psychologist to serve on a U.S. Olympic sports medicine team and was the first Asian American to head the American Psychological Association. Suinn spoke with contributing editor Robert Epstein from *Psychology Today* about the mind–body connection.

Richard Suinn

2   **PT:** How has sports psychology changed over the years?
3   **RS:** In its early days, sports psychology was mostly concerned with developing assessment methods that would identify those people with the potential to become superior athletes. Modern sports psychology, which dates from around the early 1970s, is focused on psychological training, on exercises that strengthen the mental skills that will help athletic performance. Those skills include stress management, visualization[1], goal-setting, concentration, focus, even relaxation.

_____

_____

_____

4   **PT:** Can you give us an example of how techniques are helping Olympians?
5   **RS:** I remember one case in which an Olympic boxer lost his desire to go on competing. A consultation with a sports psychologist helped him to become focused again on his goals. This is an approach that often provides the solution to issues of motivation.
6   Instead of just getting athletes "psyched up[2]," sports psychologists prefer to help them understand why they're doing what they're doing now, even though their eventual goal—say, winning a gold medal—may be a few years down the road. Goal-setting helps to bring the future a little closer by breaking it down into steps to take this week, next week, next month. That way, athletes can keep a record of their progress, keeping in mind where they're eventually going to end up. It enables those who are feeling that they want to give up to stay with the program. In the case of the boxer, he did stick with it, and he went on to compete in the Games.

_____

_____

_____

[1] **visualization** – picturing someone or something in your mind
[2] **get psyched-up** – to prepare mentally before doing something so you feel confident

7 **PT:** You've often written about a technique called "mental practice." What do you mean by that—and how does it work?

8 **RS:** Mental practice is also referred to as "visualization" or "imagery rehearsal." We start with 20 to 30 minutes of relaxation training, followed by the visualization of some aspect of the athlete's game that needs improvement. It's the mental equivalent of physical practice.

9   For instance, if your golf swing isn't perfect and your coach shows you the proper swing, then during visualization you practice making that correct swing in your mind. It may be that your muscles start to learn through this visualizing practice the proper way of moving. There is in fact research evidence that indicates that when athletes use visualization after relaxation, their performance does improve.

10   There is also evidence to suggest that if you use the wrong imagery—if you imagine yourself missing the swing or losing the game—your performance will get worse.

11 **PT:** Can the techniques you use to help athletes be applied to everyday life?

12 **RS:** Let's take stress as an example. The first thing that athletes do in dealing with their stress is to identify what triggers it. For some people, it's a particular environment in which they find themselves; for others, it's certain words that people use. The second step is to be aware of how they react when they're under stress. Sometimes they have a physiological[3] reaction, such as sweaty palms or an elevated heart rate. In that case, we have them use biofeedback[4] or relaxation training. Prevention is even better: If they know that they're going to face a stressful situation, they can engage in some relaxation procedures beforehand.

13   These are all tactics that people can use in their own lives. But people should be aware that many of these exercises do take some time to learn. They have to be practiced, in the same way that athletes have to practice their physical skills.

[3] **physiological** – having to do with how the body works

[4] **biofeedback** – a technique to help you control a body function that you normally cannot control, such as heart rate or blood pressure

Comprehension Check

A Read the following statements. If a statement is true according to the article, write *T* on the line. If it is false, write *F*.

_____ 1. Sports psychology used to be concerned with developing assessment tools to identify people who could become superior athletes.

_____ 2. The purpose of sports psychology has remained the same over the years.

_____ 3. There are many mental skills that will help athletic performance.

_____ 4. Sports psychologists teach athletes how to set goals for themselves.

_____ 5. Research shows that when athletes use visualization after relaxation, their performance improves.

_____ 6. The skills that sports psychologists teach athletes can also be applied to other areas in life.

_____ 7. Most of the skills that athletes learn from sports psychologists can be learned quickly and do not need to be practiced.

_____ 8. Sweaty palms or an elevated heart rate are examples of physiological reactions.

_____ 9. *Visualization* and *imagery rehearsal* mean the same thing.

✓ **Summarizing**

B Using only your paraphrases, write a one-paragraph summary of the interview.

_____

_____

_____

_____

_____

_____

A Match each word or phrase with the correct definition.

Word or Phrase	Definition
_____ 1. potential	**a.** method
_____ 2. down the road	**b.** something considered the same as something else
_____ 3. consultation	
_____ 4. stick with it	**c.** a meeting to discuss something or to get advice
_____ 5. equivalent	**d.** to continue to do something
_____ 6. tactic	**e.** to cause something to happen
_____ 7. trigger	**f.** the ability to develop, achieve, or succeed
	g. in the future

B Complete each sentence with the correct word or phrase from Exercise A.

1. Don't give up trying to learn Japanese. If you _____, you will be able to get a job in Japan _____.

2. A mile is the _____ of about 1.6 kilometers.

3. One_____ that is useful for athletes is called *visualization*.

4. You have the _____ to become a great athlete.

5. Certain foods like chocolate _____ my headaches.

6. After a _____ with my doctor, I decided to get more exercise.

SKILL
FOR ✓
SUCCESS

Understanding Word Parts: The Prefixes *en-* and *em-*
The prefix *en-* (or *em-* before words beginning with *m*, *b*, or *p*) is used to form verbs meaning "to cause to be something" or "to put into something." In this article, you learned the word *enable*, which means "to cause someone to be able to do something" or "to make something possible."

C Add the prefix *en-* or *em-* to each word to make a new word.

1. courage	*encourage*
2. danger	
3. bitter	
4. power	
5. rich	
6. large	

D Complete each sentence below with the correct word from Exercise C. Be sure to use the correct form of the words.

1. He was _____ by his company's refusal to give him a raise.

2. She _____ her daughter to go to college.

3. Mr. Goren would never do anything to _____ the lives of his children.

4. The judge _____ the police to search the suspect's car.

5. I'm going to get this small photograph _____.

6. The farmer wants to _____ the soil with fertilizer.

Reading Poetry

Edgar A. Guest (1881–1959) was a British-born author and poet. "It Couldn't Be Done" is one of his best-loved poems.

The rhythm of "It Couldn't Be Done" is very regular and strong. Listen to your teacher read the poem out loud. Then practice reading it out loud yourself. Finally, in a small group, discuss the questions that follow the poem.

It Couldn't Be Done

by Edgar A. Guest

Somebody said that it couldn't be done,
But he with a chuckle replied
That "maybe it couldn't," but he would be one
Who wouldn't say so till he'd tried.
So he buckled right in[1] with the trace[2] of a
   grin
On his face. If he worried he hid it.
He started to sing as he tackled the thing
That couldn't be done, and he did it.

Somebody scoffed[3]: "Oh, you'll never do
   that;
At least no one ever has done it";
But he took off his coat and he took off his
   hat,
And the first thing we knew he'd begun it.
With a lift of his chin and a bit of a grin,
Without any doubting or quiddit[4],
He started to sing as he tackled the thing
That couldn't be done, and he did it.

There are thousands to tell you it cannot be
   done,
There are thousands to prophesy failure;
There are thousands to point out to you, one
   by one,
The dangers that await to assail[5] you.
But just buckle in with a bit of a grin,
Just take off your coat and go to it;
Just start to sing as you tackle the thing
That "cannot be done," and you'll do it.

---

[1] **buckle in** – to start to do something right away

[2] **trace** – a small amount of something

[3] **scoff** – to laugh at a person or an idea

[4] **quiddit** – (obsolete) quibble; an argument over something unimportant

[5] **assail** – to attack

1. How would you describe the tone of the poem?
2. What do you think the message of the poem is? Do you agree with it?
3. Have you ever wanted to do something that other people thought was impossible? What was it? How did it turn out?
4. In the third stanza, the author says, "There are thousands to point out to you, one by one, / The dangers that wait to assail you." What dangers do you think he is talking about?
5. Throughout history, some people have opposed those with new ideas and those who want to try new things. Who can you think of that falls in this category? What kind of opposition did he or she face?

Tie It All Together

Discussion

Discuss these questions in a small group.

1. Psychiatrist Sel Lederman has said, "Any experience in life, winning or losing, is only of significance if we learn from it. Usually, we learn more from losing than from winning." Do you agree that there is more to be learned from losing than from winning? What are some life lessons that losing can teach?

2. Do you think that sports can play an important part in promoting world peace? If so, in what ways?

3. Have you ever learned something important as a result of losing or failing at something? What did you learn?

4. Discuss the following sayings about winning and losing. What do you think each one means?
   a. Don't put all your eggs in one basket.
   b. Don't count your chickens before they hatch.
   c. A bird in the hand is worth two in the bush.
   d. It's no use crying over spilled milk.
   e. It isn't whether you win or lose; it's how you play the game.
   f. Look ahead or you'll find yourself behind.

5. Do you think this cartoon is funny? Why or why not? Write a caption for the cartoon.

Drawing by Chas. Addams; © 1940, 1968 The New Yorker Magazine, Inc.

Find and circle the names of 14 popular sports. The words may be horizontal, vertical, or diagonal. One word has been found for you.

archery	~~diving~~	karate
baseball	hockey	skiing
basketball	horseracing	swimming
bicycling	ice skating	volleyball
crew	judo	

```
S R X S Y G Z H I Q S A U T J W K V A L M E N O O D
T A D V X A M E R D W C R A A R A N L A Z Y T R B I
L S K I I N G I N S I B E C E V O L L E Y B A L L M
I K U W V D N E D O M I T T H L P Q R S G O O B S G
N B B C Y I E P S I M B O F T E Z Q R L S L A N N H
G L K F G I N N I S O M O B R C R W L M A I I L
D C A J H K L G O O N Y T A B C O Y E A T G L Y K K
H O R S E R A C I N G Z H E X Y C R B L E C D R I J
M J A P O S V U L T O R E D E O R T I U Y C D E E F
O E T Q R W U T W I L L I T V B E U I C C J U D O G
I C E S K A T I N G I S O B P K W K I B T I F Y I E
F P X Y Z A Z E B R A T T R S O Z B O S J A O J A A
H R I E B O B O Y S I J S A T I T H O C K E Y T I B
Q G C E N O P O P I S R B E G A D E C F B E Y O N C
S T B A S E B A L L O O B O T L A D F U G E T I N D
```

Barefoot Marathon

Chapter 2 discussed the history of the marathon, a challenging 26-mile race. In this video, you will learn about a man who runs marathons with no shoes! Can you imagine running a long distance without shoes? What would that feel like? Why do you think somebody might run this way?

A Study these words. Then watch the video.

absorb	cushion	lost touch
arch	endure	strike the ground
barefoot	impact	vulnerable

B Read these sentences and then watch the video again. Circle the sentence that best describes the main idea.

1. If you want to start running barefoot, you have to change the way you run—striking the ground with the middle or front of your foot before the heel.

2. Recent research supports the idea that our feet were designed to function best without shoes, something Ken Bob Saxton already knows.

3. Irene Davis believes that wearing shoes has made the muscles in our feet weaker and more prone to injury.

C Discuss this question with a partner or in a small group.

There is a saying, "It is not the destination that matters, but the journey that counts." Do you think that Ken Bob Saxton would agree or disagree with this statement? Do you agree or disagree?

Reader's Journal

Think about the topics and ideas you have read about and discussed in this unit. Pick a topic from the list, choose one of the discussion questions in the unit, or write about an idea of your own. Write about it for ten to twenty minutes.

• competition
• a sports hero you admire
• traditional sports in your country
• what makes someone a good role model

Vocabulary Self-Test

Complete each sentence with the correct word or phrase.

A down the road   keep her cool   stick with it
    equivalent   mentor   take it in stride
    high-profile   potential

1. We plan to open another store sometime _____.

2. It's a very good plan. I think you should _____.

3. We hired a(n) _____ lawyer to defend us. All our friends recommended him.

4. I've learned so much from my acting teacher. She's been my _____ for years.

5. He's doing the _____ job at the new store, but he's making more money and working fewer hours.

6. My nephew has the _____ to become a great athlete. He just has to keep practicing.

7. She never loses her temper. She can _____ even in times of stress.

8. You're a politician. You get lots of criticism, and you'll just have to _____.

B cheered   get caught up in   spectators
    distracted   perseverance   tactics
    flaw

1. It's hard not to _____ the glory of winning.

2. All of the _____ at the circus loved the performance of the animals and their trainers. When it was over, they all clapped and _____.

3. Without hard work and _____, I don't think you will accomplish your goal.

4. Her biggest _____ is that she acts too proud and looks down on others.

5. It's easy to get _____ from your homework with the TV on.

6. What _____ do you plan to use to win the election?

C collapse   exhaustion   trigger

consultation   running neck and neck   triumph

delight   suspense

1. I worked hard in the hot sun all day. Now I feel like I'm going to _____ from _____.

2. The children smiled in _____ when they saw the new puppy their father brought home.

3. After his _____ with a psychologist, he learned how to manage his stress.

4. The book describes her _____ over the many tragedies in her life.

5. We waited in _____ for the winner of the election to be announced.

6. Sometimes stress can _____ a stomachache.

7. The two runners from Japan were _____ for most of the race.

HEALING POWER

Did you know that listening to music can help heal sick people? Eating certain plants can also help improve health. In this unit, you will read about some interesting new discoveries (and some old ones) in the world of medicine.

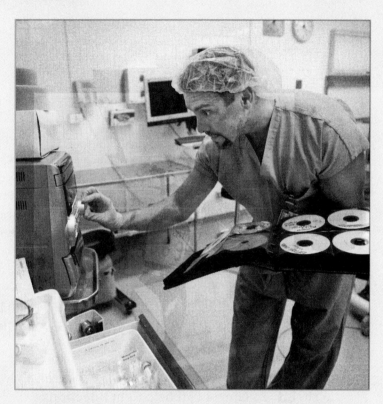

Points to Ponder

Think about these questions and discuss them in a small group.

1. Do you think certain foods are healthy? Which ones?
2. What foods do you eat when you are sick?
3. Do you eat or drink anything on a regular basis to keep healthy? Do you take vitamins? Do you exercise? If so, how often?
4. Do you think music can help heal sick people? How?

Plant Power

Before You Read

A Discuss these questions with a partner.

1. Do you like spicy food? Do you think spicy food can make you feel better?
2. Do you drink any kind of herbal teas when you have a cold? A stomachache? A headache? A sore throat?
3. Do you believe in the health benefits of certain plants? Which ones?

✓ **Using Background Knowledge**

B Think about what you know about the health benefits of certain plants. Check (✔) the statements you agree with. Then compare answers with a partner.

❑ 1. Using plants to prevent and treat illnesses is a new idea.
❑ 2. Ginger can help fight infections.
❑ 3. Many people drink tea for medicinal purposes.
❑ 4. Chile peppers are healthy.
❑ 5. People have used garlic to treat diseases for thousands of years.
❑ 6. Only a few kinds of plants are used as medicine.
❑ 7. Scientists often discover new medicinal uses for plants.

C Learn the meanings of the following words before you read the article.

medicinal (1)	therapeutic (7)	potent (8)
well-being (4)	promoted (8)	stimulate (8)
affectionately (7)	remedy (8)	

Plant Power

1   The use of plants to prevent and cure diseases is nothing new. Most ancient cultures and many modern ones believe in the medicinal benefits of certain plants.

Chile Pepper Prescription

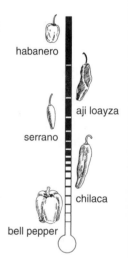

2   Have you ever bitten into a chile pepper? Your eyes start to water. You sniffle. You cough. You sweat. Your heart beats fast. Your lips, tongue, and mouth burn. That's because chile peppers are so hot. Chile peppers are the fruit of the plant capsicum. What makes them so hot is a chemical called capsaicin, an oil that is not found in any other plant. It is colorless and odorless, but very strong. If you put 1 drop of capsaicin oil into 100,000 drops of water and drank it, you would still really feel the heat.

The Scoville scale

3   Some chile peppers are hotter than others. The extra heat has to do with the type, not the amount, of capsaicin oil. Luckily, biting into a pepper isn't the only way to tell how hot a pepper is. A machine can measure the heat of a pepper's capsaicin. The measurements are called Scoville units (named for the man who invented the test). The more Scoville units, the hotter the pepper. A jalapeño pepper measures between 3,500 and 4,500 units. The habanero is one of the hottest chile peppers in the world. It goes off the scale at 350,000 units.

4   Chile peppers are added to many foods. They're in salsa—the red sauce you dip tortilla chips in. They're also in Tabasco sauce, chili con carne, and spicy chicken wings. No matter how you eat them, chiles make you feel good. The capsaicin releases chemicals in the brain called endorphins, which give you a feeling of well-being.

5   Chile peppers are very healthy. They are packed with vitamins A and D. For centuries, people all over the world have used chiles to treat head colds, flu, and asthma. Capsaicin is also a natural pain reliever. Whether eaten in chile peppers or used to make creams, capsaicin helps reduce pain in diseases such as arthritis and diabetes. It can even be used to stop itching. Some people rub diluted[1] capsaicin oil on their gums to stop toothaches.

6   Scientists are also studying the use of capsaicin in other illnesses, such as headaches. Research shows that it may also reduce the chance of developing

---

[1] **diluted** – refers to a liquid made weaker or thinner by mixing another liquid with it

some types of cancer. Not only do chile peppers make people feel better, they make them feel cooler, too. Eating a chile pepper causes your face and scalp to sweat—and sweating helps you chill out. That's why chile peppers are popular in countries with hot climates.

Garlic May Stink, but It Can Help

7   Chiles aren't the only plants that can make you feel better. In fact, the medicinal powers of garlic have been praised for thousands of years. It is affectionately called "the stinking rose" because of its many therapeutic benefits. Garlic is one of the oldest known medicinal plants, and it has been credited with fighting off infections, lowering blood pressure and blood sugar, and preventing colds. Current research suggests that garlic may also help prevent some forms of cancer, heart disease, and strokes. The Chinese and Japanese have used garlic for centuries to treat high blood pressure. In fact, the Japanese Food and Drug Administration officially named garlic as a treatment for this condition. The Japanese have also found evidence that garlic may be helpful in treating stomach ulcers.

Ginger: A Universal Medicine

8   Ginger has been a favorite ingredient in Asian cooking for thousands of years. It has a strong, spicy, and sweet flavor that is added to many dishes. Today, people around the world use ginger to make breads, pickles, soft drinks, and desserts. But ginger can also be used to prevent and fight disease. In fact, ginger has been called the "universal medicine." Using ginger to cure what ails you is nothing new. For over 2,000 years, Chinese doctors have promoted the use of ginger to treat many health problems. Ginger is a well-known remedy for preventing nausea[2], especially morning sickness[3] and motion sickness[4]. It also aids digestion. Ginger contains very potent anti-inflammatory compounds called gingerols. These substances help to relax blood vessels and stimulate blood flow. Therefore, consuming ginger may help to lower blood pressure and reduce blood clotting. It also stimulates blood circulation and reduces fever. In addition, ginger has been found to fight colds and cleanse the kidneys. Finally, some people use ginger to soothe painful joints and cure skin infections.

A Cup of Tea May Cure You

9   Tea is one of the most popular drinks all over the world, but it is also a strong medicinal herb. The Chinese have been drinking tea since 3000 B.C. and believe it helps digestion. Green tea, which is also popular in Japan, is rich in fluoride and can prevent tooth decay. Green tea has also been shown to fight skin and stomach cancer and help the immune system. People in some cultures put wet green tea

---

[2] **nausea** – the feeling you have when you think you are going to vomit

[3] **morning sickness** – the feeling of nausea that some women have when they are pregnant

[4] **motion sickness** – the feeling of nausea that some people have when riding in a moving vehicle

leaves on insect bites to reduce itching. Oolong tea is drunk in Korea and other Asian countries to reduce cholesterol[5] levels after a fatty meal. Japanese research suggests that oolong tea may help lower blood pressure and limit the risk of diseases of the blood vessels.

10   Not only does the age-old use of chile peppers, garlic, ginger, and tea continue today to help cure illnesses, but more than 80,000 other species of plants are also used throughout the world as medicine. Scientists and doctors in many countries are discovering new medicinal uses for plants all the time.

---

[5] **cholesterol** – a substance in fat, blood, and other cells in your body that can sometimes cause heart disease

After You Read

Comprehension Check

A Read these statements. If a statement is true according to the article, write *T* on the line. If it is false, write *F*.

Americans consume more than 250 million pounds of garlic annually.

_____ 1.   Modern cultures rarely use plants to help cure illnesses.

_____ 2.   Eating a chile pepper is the only way to see how hot it is.

_____ 3.   Chile peppers are used in many kinds of foods.

_____ 4.   Capsaicin is found in many kinds of plants.

_____ 5.   Chile peppers have a lot of vitamins A and D.

_____ 6.   Chile peppers are more popular in cold climates than in hot ones.

_____ 7.   Garlic is one of the oldest known medicinal plants.

_____ 8.   Chinese medicine has long recommended ginger to treat many health problems.

_____ 9.   Gingerols help to relax blood vessels and stimulate blood flow.

_____ 10.   People drink oolong tea to increase cholesterol levels.

SKILL FOR SUCCESS ✓

Taking Notes
Taking notes is a good way to help you understand and remember what you read. There are many ways to take notes. One way is to take "two-column notes." When you take two-column notes, you write the topic or main idea in the left column and supporting information (such as details or examples) in the right column.

B Read the article again. This time, take notes on the health benefits of chile peppers, garlic, ginger, and tea.

Food	Health Benefits
1. Chile peppers	−Treat head colds, flu, and asthma
	−Used as a natural pain reliever
	−Help reduce pain in arthritis and diabetes
	−Stop itching
	−May reduce the chance of developing some types of cancer
2. Garlic	
3. Ginger	
4. Green tea	
5. Oolong tea	

A Circle the correct answer.

1. If you believe that green tea has <u>medicinal</u> value, you _____.
   a. think it is good for you   b. think it is unhealthy

2. If someone smiles <u>affectionately</u> at you, it probably means _____.
   a. she likes you
   b. she disapproves of you

3. If you find gardening a <u>therapeutic</u> activity, you _____.
   a. feel more relaxed and healthier when you do it
   b. feel angry because you have to do it

4. If your mother feeds you chicken soup as a <u>remedy</u> for a cold, she thinks it will _____.
   a. make you feel worse
   b. make you feel better

5. If you take medicine to <u>stimulate</u> your heart rate, you want it to _____.
   a. slow down
   b. speed up

6. If a spice is very <u>potent</u>, you would probably add _____ of it if you want your food to be milder.
   a. more
   b. less

7. Doctors who <u>promote</u> regular exercise to stay healthy _____.
   a. encourage their patients to exercise
   b. don't want their patients to exercise

8. Which would be more likely to improve your sense of <u>well-being</u>?
   a. listening to your favorite music
   b. having a nightmare

✓ Learning Synonyms and Antonyms

B For each pair of words, circle S if they are synonyms or A if they are antonyms.

1. potent	weak	S	A
2. medicinal	therapeutic	S	A
3. potent	powerful	S	A
4. risk	danger	S	A
5. affectionately	lovingly	S	A
6. stimulate	encourage	S	A
7. remedy	cure	S	A
8. promote	oppose	S	A

SKILL FOR SUCCESS

Understanding Word Parts: The Suffix -*less*

The **suffix** -*less* is often added to words to mean "without." In this chapter, you learned that capsaicin is *colorless* and *odorless*. This means that capsaicin has no color or odor.

C Read the sentences and write a definition for each underlined word.

One out of every four people in the world eats chiles every day.

1. Her grandfather is a rich man today. But when he first came to this country, he was <u>penniless</u>.

   _____

2. Our cat is <u>fearless</u>. Even big dogs don't scare her.

   _____

3. My car went out of control on the icy street, and I was <u>powerless</u> to stop it.

   _____

4. The <u>childless</u> couple has been trying to adopt a baby for many years.

   _____

5. After I heard the news, I was so surprised that I was <u>speechless</u>.

   _____

Talk It Over

Discuss these questions as a class.

1. Do you think there are any dangers in using plants as medicines? If so, what kinds of dangers?
2. Besides the plants mentioned in the article, what other plants do you know of that can be used for medicinal purposes?

Music's Surprising Power to Heal

Before You Read

A Discuss these questions with a partner.

1. Do you ever listen to music to make you feel better when you are sick? What kind of music makes you feel better?
2. Do you listen to music to help relax when you are feeling stressed? What kind of music?

✓ **Skimming for the Main Idea**

B Skim the article one time. Circle the correct answer.

1. What is the article about?
   a. ways music can help sick people
   b. mental and emotional disabilities

2. What is the aim of the article?
   a. to inform the reader about the therapeutic benefits of music
   b. to entertain the reader with amusing stories

3. The article lists _____.
   a. the best kinds of music to play in hospitals
   b. key areas where music therapy is effective

C Learn the meanings of the following words and phrase before you read the article.

hooked up to (1)   supplemental (4)   moderate (9)
recovering (1)   straight (5)   distinguished (10)
enhances (2)   disorders (9)

Music's Surprising Power to Heal

by David M. Mazie

1   Soon after Marianne Strebely was severely injured in a car accident, she lay on a bed in the operating room of St. Luke's Hospital in Cleveland, Ohio, surrounded by a team of doctors. Strebely was hooked up to a computer that checked her heart and brain. She was also hooked up, by earphones, to a tape recorder playing music. During the surgery, the doctors listened to music from another tape recorder. Strebely's doctor, Clyde L. Nash, said, "Music reduces tension in the operating room and also helps relax the patient. The music is better than medication." After the surgery, Strebely said, "I remained calm before the operation and didn't need as much sedation[1]." When she was at home recovering from the surgery, Strebely listened to more music. She didn't even need to take the medicine her doctor gave her to help the pain.

> *"Music reduces tension in the operating room and also helps relax the patient. The music is better than medication."*

2   Nash is one of many doctors who believe that when music is combined with conventional treatments, it can help heal sick people. Dr. Mathew H. M. Lee, director of the Rusk Rehabilitation Institute in New York, believes in the benefits of music, too. He thinks music helps to avoid serious complications during illness. It also enhances patients' well-being and shortens their hospital stays.

How Music Helps

3   How does music help? Music seems to trigger certain physical responses. Some studies show, for example, that music can lower blood pressure and metabolism[2] and respiration rates, which helps the body's ability to respond to stress. Other studies suggest that music helps increase the production of natural pain relievers called endorphins. Music may also help the body produce a chemical called salivary immunoglobulin, which speeds healing and fights infection.

4   One study took place at California State University, where psychologist Janet Lapp studied 30 people who suffered from migraine[3] headaches for five weeks. One group of the people listened to their favorite music; a second group used relaxation techniques; a third group did neither. All three groups received similar medication. Music proved the most effective supplemental

---

[1] **sedation** – use of a drug that makes a person or animal sleepy or calm

[2] **metabolism** – the chemical processes in your body that change food into the energy you need

[3] **migraine** – an extremely bad headache

therapy, especially over the long term. A year later, the patients who had continued to listen to music reported one-sixth as many headaches as before; these were also less severe and ended more quickly. Lapp believes music can be very helpful for people who suffer from migraine headaches.

5   In another study at Baltimore's St. Agnes Hospital, classical music was played in the critical-care units. "Half an hour of music produced the same effect as 10 milligrams of Valium[4]," says Dr. Raymond Bahr, head of the coronary-care unit. "Some patients who had been awake for three or four straight days were able to go into a deep sleep."

6   Music therapy is proving especially effective in several key medical areas:

• *Pain, anxiety, and depression*. Research shows that music can help people cope with physical pain. "When I had my first baby," says Susan Koletsky of Shaker Heights, Ohio, "I was in difficult labor for two days. The second time around, I wanted to avoid the pain." When she had her second baby, Susan listened to relaxing jazz in the delivery room. She also listened to classical music by Bach and Beethoven. "The music produced a much easier experience," she claims.

7   Music can also help fight depression. Patients are often depressed, refusing to talk with doctors and nurses. "The music therapist can give them a positive outlook," says Dr. Nathan A. Berger, director of the Ireland Cancer Center in Cleveland. "That makes it easier to communicate and encourages patients to cooperate more in their treatment."

8   Cancer patients often stay in their hospital rooms, dwelling on their problems, refusing to talk with doctors and nurses. Music helped a 17-year-old patient at the center. The patient, named Ginny, had skin damage from cancer treatments. When music therapist Deforia Lane saw her, Ginny was withdrawn[5] and silent, sitting in a wheelchair. Lane gave her a quick music lesson in the omnichord, a small instrument. Then they played and sang together for 45 minutes. After the session, the patient's mother told Lane in a voice full of emotion, "This is the first time Ginny has shown any happiness since she walked into this hospital."

9   • *Mental, physical, and emotional disabilities*. The Ivymount School in Rockville, Maryland, helps children with developmental disorders ranging from emotional problems to mental retardation, autism, and severe to moderate learning disabilities. Ruthlee Adler, a music therapist, uses song and dance to help the children learn—and cope. "While the seriously handicapped may ignore other kinds of stimulation, they respond to music," she says.

10   • *Neurological disorders*. Dr. Oliver Sacks is a distinguished neurologist. He reports that patients with neurological disorders who cannot talk or move are often able to sing and sometimes even dance. "The power of music is remarkable in such people," Sacks observes. Consider the example of a 70-year-old stroke[6] patient at Beth Abraham

---

[4] **Valium** – the brand name of a drug that makes a person or animal calm or unconscious

[5] **withdrawn** – quiet and not willing to be around other people

[6] **stroke** – a sudden decrease in the blood supply to the brain, which can cause a loss of consciousness, movement, or speech

Hospital in New York City. In group sessions for elderly patients, he always sat by himself, never speaking. One day, when therapist Connie Tomaino played an old folk song, the man started to hum. Tomaino played the tune regularly after that. Finally, the man sang some of the words. "Before you knew it," says Tomaino, "he was talking."

11   Michael Thaut is the director of Colorado State University's Center for Biomedical Research in Music. He tested ten stroke victims for four weeks to see how music affected their ability to walk smoothly. First he measured the timing of their strides[7] without music. Then he measured the timing of their strides as they walked to music. He noticed a significant improvement when the patients walked to musical accompaniment. "In almost every case," says Thaut, "the timing of the stride improved with music."

12   Music's therapeutic benefits, of course, aren't confined to those who are ill. "Apart from the simple enjoyment that music provides, we're learning how much it can also help us in our daily personal lives," says Ireland Cancer Center's Dr. Berger. To "psych up" for important presentations and meetings, Berger hums the theme music from the movie *Rocky* or from the opera *Aida*. "Music can also act as a tension- or pain-reliever for something as routine as going to the dentist," he says, "or it can simply give expression to our moods."

13   To gain the full benefit of music, you need to work it into your daily schedule. During his lunch hour, Jeffrey Scheffel closes his office door at the Mayo Clinic in Rochester, Minnesota, puts on a pair of earphones, and, leaning back in his desk chair, tunes in some light jazz or Mozart, depending on the mood he wants to build. "It rejuvenates[8] me," explains Scheffel, research administrator at the famed medical center. "It gives my brain a break, lets me focus on something else for a few minutes, and helps me get through the rest of the day."

14   Few people understand the therapeutic powers of music better than Cleveland music therapist Deforia Lane. Ten years ago, during her own bout with cancer, singing helped her relax and take her mind off the disease. Since then, she has used that experience to help others. "Music is not magic," says Ms. Lane with a warm smile and rich soprano voice. "But in a hospital or at home, for young people or older ones, it can be a potent medicine that helps us all." ■

---

[7] **stride** – the step you take when you walk

[8] **rejuvenate** – to make someone feel young and strong again

After You Read

Comprehension Check

A Circle the correct answer.

1. Both Dr. Nash and Dr. Lee _____.
   a. practice medicine in Ohio
   b. believe in the medical benefits of music
   c. were members of Marianne Strebely's surgical team

2. Music therapist Deforia Lane believes that music _____.
   a. works like magic
   b. can be a strong medicine
   c. cannot help depressed people

3. Which is NOT mentioned as a medical area where music therapy is proving effective?
   a. neurological disorders
   b. mental and emotional disabilities
   c. broken arms and legs

4. From the article, you can infer that _____.
   a. music is only good for entertainment
   b. both doctors and patients benefit from music
   c. music is better than traditional treatments

5. Which of the following speeds healing and fights infection?
   a. a chemical called salivary immunoglobulin
   b. natural pain relievers called endorphins
   c. a small instrument called the omnichord

6. Music helped a 70-year-old stroke patient at Beth Abraham Hospital _____.
   a. walk again
   b. start talking again
   c. learn to sing and dance

7. What kind of students attend the Ivymount School?
   a. children who are very musical
   b. only children who have moderate learning disabilities
   c. children with different types of developmental problems

SKILL FOR SUCCESS

Identifying Supporting Information: Quoting Experts
Authors often **quote experts** to support their ideas. In the article "Music's Surprising Power to Heal," the author quotes experts in medicine and music therapy to support his ideas about the therapeutic benefits of music.

B Complete the chart with the names, occupations, and quotes of the experts.

Name	Occupation	Quote
1. Dr. Clyde L. Nash	Doctor	
2.	Doctor	"Music helps to avoid serious complications during illness. It also enhances patients' well-being and shortens their hospital stays."
3. Janet Lapp		"Music can be very helpful for people who suffer from migraine headaches."
4. Deforia Lane	Music therapist	
5. Ruthlee Adler		"While the seriously handicapped may ignore other kinds of stimulation, they respond to music."
6.	Neurologist	"The power of music is remarkable in [patients with neurological disorders]."
7.	Research administrator	
8.	Doctor	"Music can also act as a tension- or pain-reliever for something as routine as going to the dentist, or it can simply give expression to our moods."

SKILL FOR SUCCESS

Understanding Anecdotes

Anecdotes are short accounts or stories about something that happened to someone. Anecdotes are often used in introductions because they grab the reader's attention. Authors also use anecdotes to support their ideas. The author of the article used several anecdotes.

C Answer these questions.

1. What anecdote did the author use in the introduction? Do you think it was an effective way to begin the article? Why or why not?

    _____

    _____

2. Why did the author include the anecdote about Ginny?

    _____

    _____

3. Why did the author include the anecdote about the 70-year-old stroke patient?

    _____

    _____

✓ **Summarizing**

D The author described several scientific studies in the article. Using your own words, summarize the studies.

1. Janet Lapp's study of 30 people who suffered from migraine headaches

    _____

    _____

    _____

2. Michael Thaut's study of ten stroke victims

    _____

    _____

    _____

Vocabulary Practice

A Cross out the word or phrase in each group that does not belong.

1. connected to	hooked up to	plugged into	removed from
2. recovering	improving	feeling worse	getting better
3. moderate	severe	extreme	acute
4. helps	enhances	forgets	improves
5. supplemental	primary	additional	extra
6. consecutive	straight	out of order	in a row
7. disorder	theory	illness	sickness
8. eminent	famous	distinguished	ordinary

B Circle the correct answer.

1. If you worked for nine <u>straight</u> days, you _____.
   a. worked all nine days
   b. worked some of the nine days

2. Which would you use to <u>enhance</u> the flavor of food?
   a. water
   b. spices

3. A <u>distinguished</u> professor of history _____.
   a. knows a lot about history
   b. doesn't know very much about history

4. Which would be an example of <u>supplemental</u> income?
   a. the money you make from your job
   b. extra money your parents give you for your birthday

5. Which would you <u>hook up to</u> a computer?
   a. speakers
   b. paper

6. Which is an example of a physical <u>disorder</u>?
   a. a good sense of humor
   b. severe stomachaches

7. If the patient is still <u>recovering</u> after his surgery, he is _____.
   a. completely healed
   b. not completely better yet

8. If there is a <u>moderate</u> increase in unemployment, the increase is _____.
   a. not extreme
   b. extreme

SKILL FOR SUCCESS

Understanding Word Parts: The Prefix *dis-*
The prefix *dis-* is added to the beginning of some words to form their opposites. For example, in this chapter, you saw the word *disability*.

C Circle the correct answer. Use your dictionary to help you.

1. I tried to _____ her from leaving the party so early.
   a. disobey
   b. displease
   c. disillusion
   d. dissuade

2. Although we _____ about the cause of the problem, we both wanted the same solution.
   a. disapproved
   b. displeased
   c. disagreed
   d. disillusioned

3. He pretends to be truthful, but he is actually very _____.
   a. disorganized
   b. dishonest
   c. disillusioned
   d. disobeyed

4. He was punished because he _____ the rules.
   a. disobeyed
   b. dissuaded
   c. disillusioned
   d. displeased

5. We thought our sister's nasty book about our family was _____ to our parents.
   a. disabled
   b. dissatisfied
   c. disillusioned
   d. disloyal

6. I was _____ and disappointed when I learned the unpleasant truth about the mayor. I never thought he would do something so immoral.
   a. disagreed
   b. dissuaded
   c. disillusioned
   d. disobeyed

Talk it Over

Discuss these questions as a class.

1. Have you or has anyone you know ever had any personal experiences with the healing power of music?
2. If you were feeling sick or recovering from surgery, what kind of music would you like to listen to?

UNIT 5

CHAPTER 3

Frogs and Human Health

Before You Read

A Discuss these questions with a partner.

1. What steps are being taken to protect plants and animals in your country?
2. Which animals do you think are important to medical research?

✓ **Skimming for the Main Idea**

B Skim the article one time. Circle the correct answer.

The article mainly discusses _____.
   a. the differences between dart-poison frogs and aquatic frogs
   b. the ways frogs can benefit human health
   c. the reproductive method of frogs
   d. the biological diversity of the rain forest

C Learn the meanings of the following words before you read the article.

adaptations (1)   toxins (3)   wounds (5)
combat (1)   defenses (3)   beneficial (5)
predators (2)   unpalatable (3)

What is the relationship between frogs and human health? Scientists around the world have discovered that many frogs produce chemicals that could be used in making human medicines. Unfortunately for humans, some species of frogs are dying out before we can study them for their medical value.

Frogs and Human Health

by Bill Sharp

1   Scientists are interested in studying frogs because frogs have developed unique chemical adaptations that make them valuable helpers in the search for new, more effective medicines to treat many human ailments such as ulcers, arthritis, and burns. The medicines could also be used to combat heart diseases, neurological diseases, and extreme pain. Unfortunately, many species of frogs are dying out before scientists have time to fully explore their medicinal potential.

2   Queensland frogs are an example of a missed medical opportunity because of the loss of a species. These frogs once lived in the rain forests of Australia. They had a unique form of reproduction. Female frogs swallowed their eggs, protecting them from predators. The baby frogs developed in the mother's stomach until they were big enough to survive. The eggs were coated with a special chemical called *prostaglandin* that shut down the mother's digestive system. Studying this reproductive method promised to offer help for people with digestive disorders, but work came to an end when the frogs became extinct in 1980.

3   The most medically interesting frogs are the dart-poison frogs of Central and South America. These small, brightly colored forest frogs got their name because for generations Colombian Indians used the toxins from the skins of these frogs to poison the tips of their darts. Unlike aquatic[1] frogs, who can escape quickly to the safety of nearby water, terrestrial[2] frogs like the dart-poison frogs have developed chemical defenses for protection. One defense is their ability to produce bad-tasting (and deadly) chemicals, thus making them extremely unpalatable to predators.

4   John Daly of the National Institutes of Health (NIH) in Bethesda, Maryland, has studied dart-poison frogs for many years. He uses the toxic chemicals found in the skin of these frogs to do research on human nerve and muscle function. One chemical he found on the skin of Ecuadorian dart-poison frogs has 200 times the pain-killing power of

[1] **aquatic** – living or happening in the water
[2] **terrestrial** – living or happening on land

morphine[3]. Drugs based on this discovery are being developed at several drug companies. Because they are a niche species in tropical forests that are dwindling daily, all of the 100 species of dart-poison frogs, along with the information they represent, are threatened by rain-forest destruction.

5   Many other kinds of frogs are threatened with extinction, too. Scientists are doing research on the endangered Houston toad because it produces a chemical similar to digitalis (a drug that strengthens the heart) that may benefit patients with heart problems. Chemicals with antibiotic properties from another endangered frog are also important in medical research. These chemicals are the basis of products being developed to treat wounds and burns. Other chemicals from endangered frogs may be beneficial in regulating appetite and body temperature.

6   Scientists around the world are worried about the effect of the loss of frogs and other endangered animals and plants. Eric Chivian is the founder and director of the Center for Health and the Global Environment at Harvard Medical School. He believes, "The current loss of biological diversity represents nothing less than a medical emergency and would demand that efforts to preserve species and ecosystems be given the highest priority."

7   Thomas Eisner, professor of biology at Cornell University, says, "For 30 years, I've been doing nothing but searching for chemicals in nature. It makes me very aware of what we don't know. When we lose species, we are destroying our legacy. Our biggest source of biochemical information for the future is what is recorded in nature." As Eisner and others have noted, when we destroy a species, we are burning an irreplaceable book of information.   ■

[3] **morphine** – a very strong drug used for stopping pain

After You Read

Comprehension Check

A Circle the correct answer.

1. According to the author, frogs are helpful in the development of new medicines because of their _____.
   a. unique chemical adaptations
   b. physical agility
   c. dwindling numbers
   d. reproductive methods

2. According to the article, dart-poison frogs are threatened by _____.
   a. toxins from their skins
   b. inability to control their body temperature
   c. biochemical information
   d. destruction of the rain forest

3. It can be inferred from the article that terrestrial frogs are _____.
   a. found mainly in Australia
   b. less interesting to medical researchers than aquatic frogs
   c. becoming extinct more quickly than aquatic frogs
   d. unable to survive completely in the water

4. Chemicals produced by the endangered Houston toad may _____.
   a. help heart patients
   b. regulate appetite
   c. treat burn victims
   d. help research on human nerves

5. Dart-poison frogs are an example of _____.
   a. endangered Houston toads
   b. terrestrial frogs
   c. aquatic frogs
   d. Queensland frogs

6. Why were scientists interested in studying the reproductive method of Queensland frogs?
   a. because the frogs became extinct
   b. because it would help people with digestive disorders
   c. in order to do research on human nerve and muscle function
   d. because they produced foul-tasting and deadly secretions

7. Which of the following is NOT mentioned as an area of research on chemicals produced by frogs and toads?
   a. heart disease
   b. nerve and muscle functions
   c. drug addiction
   d. arthritis

8. The article supports which of the following conclusions?
   a. Efforts to preserve species and ecosystems must be given a high priority.
   b. The loss of biological diversity is less important now than it was 50 years ago.
   c. The inability of frogs to adapt to their environment lessens their research value.
   d. Too much money is being spent on research into the medical benefits of frogs.

✓ Paraphrasing

B The author of this article also used quotes from experts to support his ideas. Sometimes these statements are difficult to understand. Paraphrasing them will help you understand them more easily. Paraphrase the following quotes from the article. Then compare paraphrases with a partner.

1. Eric Chivian states, "The current loss of biological diversity represents nothing less than a medical emergency and would demand that efforts to preserve species and ecosystems be given the highest priority."

   _____
   _____
   _____

2. Professor Thomas Eisner says, "For 30 years, I've been doing nothing but searching for chemicals in nature. It makes me very aware of what we don't know. When we lose species, we are destroying our legacy. Our biggest source of biochemical information for the future is what is recorded in nature."

   _____
   _____
   _____

SKILL
FOR ✓
SUCCESS

Understanding Cause and Effect

When you read, it is often important to understand the **causes** and/or **effects** of an event. When you want to find the causes (reasons), ask yourself, "Why did the event happen?" When you are looking for the effects (results), ask yourself, "What happened because of the event?"

As you read, look for these words and phrases that signal cause-and-effect relationships:

as a result	consequence(s)	therefore
because	consequently	thus
bring about	due to	
cause(s)	effect(s)	

C Answer the questions about causes and effects with information from the article.

1. Why are scientists and doctors so interested in studying frogs?

    _____

    _____

2. Why did female Queensland frogs swallow their eggs?

    _____

    _____

3. Why did research on Queensland frogs come to an end?

    _____

    _____

4. Why do dart-poison frogs produce bad-tasting chemicals?

    _____

    _____

5. Why are scientists doing research on the endangered Houston toad?

    _____

    _____

Vocabulary Practice

A Match each word with the correct definition.

Word	**Definition**
_____ **1.** wound	**a.** poisonous substances
_____ **2.** beneficial	**b.** things that provide protection against attack
_____ **3.** combat	**c.** producing a good effect
_____ **4.** predator	**d.** a deep injury to the skin
_____ **5.** toxins	**e.** to try to stop something unpleasant or harmful from happening
_____ **6.** adaptations	**f.** an animal that hunts and eats other animals in order to survive
_____ **7.** defenses	**g.** physical characteristics that have evolved to allow plants and animals to survive in their environment
_____ **8.** unpalatable	**h.** unpleasant to taste or eat

B Ask and answer these questions with a partner.

1. What <u>defenses</u> do certain frogs have that protect them from <u>predators</u>?
2. What do you do that is <u>beneficial</u> to your health?
3. What are some ways to <u>combat</u> childhood diseases?
4. Have you ever had a serious <u>wound</u>? How did you get it?
5. Why do some animals produce <u>toxins</u>?
6. What do you think is the most important <u>adaptation</u> that humans have developed?
7. What foods do you find <u>unpalatable</u>?

SKILL FOR SUCCESS

Learning Homonyms

Homonyms are words that are spelled the same or sound the same but have different meanings. Consider the word *treat*:

These medicines could <u>treat</u> ailments such as ulcers, arthritis, burns, heart disease, and extreme pain. (In this sentence, *treat* is a verb that means "to do something to improve the condition of a sick or injured person.")

If you are good, I'll give you a <u>treat</u>. (In this sentence, *treat* is a noun that means "something special you give to someone.")

Understanding the different meanings of homonyms will help you become a more fluent reader.

C Read these sentences. Write the meaning and part of speech of each underlined word. You may need to use your dictionary.

1. a. One defense is their ability to <u>produce</u> bad-tasting chemicals.
   Meaning: _____
   Part of speech: _____
   b. We like to buy fresh <u>produce</u> in the summer.
   Meaning: _____
   Part of speech: _____

2. a. Houston toads produce a chemical similar to digitalis that may <u>benefit</u> patients with heart problems.
   Meaning: _____
   Part of speech: _____
   b. The band gave a <u>benefit</u> concert to help homeless children.
   Meaning: _____
   Part of speech: _____

3. a. The eggs were <u>coated</u> with a substance called *prostaglandin*.
Meaning: _____
Part of speech: _____

    b. You need to wear a warm <u>coat</u> today.
Meaning: _____
Part of speech: _____

4. a. As many experts have <u>noted</u>, when we destroy a species, we are burning an irreplaceable book of information.
Meaning: _____
Part of speech: _____

    b. Did you send her a thank-you <u>note</u>?
Meaning: _____
Part of speech: _____

5. a. These chemicals are the basis of products being developed to treat <u>wounds</u> and burns.
Meaning: _____
Part of speech: _____

    b. She <u>wound</u> the pearl necklace around her neck.
Meaning: _____
Part of speech: _____

Talk It Over

Discuss these questions as a class.

1. Paragraph 7 of the article says, "When we destroy a species, we are burning an irreplaceable book of information." How is this true? Do you agree with this idea?
2. What other "irreplaceable books of information" might we be in danger of destroying in our fast-paced, modern lives?

Read a Prescription Label

Some medicines can only be ordered by a doctor or a dentist. These are called prescription medicines. Only a licensed pharmacist can sell prescription medicine. All prescription medicines have a label with important information.

Look at the sample label and answer the questions that follow.

Sansom Street Pharmacy - - - - - - - - - - - - - a. Pharmacy name, address, and phone
1333 SANSOM STREET, SYRACUSE, NEW YORK   number
315-555-5555

Dr. Steven Marks 516-555-1111 - - - - - - - - - - - b. Doctor's name and phone number

Date Filled **3/20/07** - - - - - - - - - - - - - - - - - c. Date prescription was filled
Rx No.: **2005112** - - - - - - - - - - - - - - - - - d. Prescription number

Samuel Roth - e. Patient's name

Lipitor Tablets, MFG: Pfizer - - - - - - - - - - - - f. Name of the medication
                            - - - - - - - - - - - - - g. MFG: Manufacturer of the medication

Dose: Take one tablet by mouth, daily- - - h. Dose: How often and when to take the
                                                 medication

QTY: 30 - i. QTY: Quantity or how much is in the
                                                 package

REFILLS 2 BEFORE 6/09/07 - - - - - - - - - - - j. Refills: The number of refills permitted
Exp. Date 1/30/09 - - - - - - - - - - - - - - - - - k. Expiration date: Do not use the
                                                 medication past this date.

The label may also have additional information, such as the following:

- Safe storage instructions, such as "Keep refrigerated"
- Instructions for use, such as "Shake well before using" or "Take before eating"
- Information about possible side effects, such as "May cause drowsiness"

1. What is the name of the pharmacy?_____
2. Who prescribed the medicine?_____
3. What is the name of the medicine? _____
4. Who is the medicine for? _____
5. How many pills are in the bottle? _____
6. How often should the patient take this medicine? _____
7. What is the prescription number? _____

Tie It All Together

Discussion

Discuss these questions in a small group.

1. Health-care professionals want people to practice more preventive medicine in their lives. What can we do to take better care of our health?

2. What foods do you think are healthy? Do you try to eat healthy foods? What foods do you think are unhealthy?

3. Make notes on the popular (traditional) treatments used in your country for the following diseases and ailments. Then share your ideas.

   a. headaches

   _____
   _____

   b. colds

   _____
   _____

   c. insomnia

   _____
   _____

   d. toothaches

   _____
   _____

   e. fevers

   _____
   _____

   f. stomachaches

   _____
   _____

   g. arthritis

   _____
   _____

   h. stress

   _____
   _____

Complete the crossword puzzle with words from the unit.

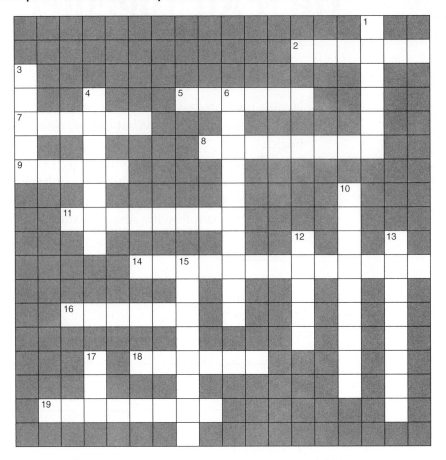

ACROSS

2. A cure

5. The stinking rose

7. A kind of tea that may help lower blood pressure

8. Name of scale that measures hotness of peppers

9. The red sauce you dip tortilla chips in

11. A short, often personal account of an event

14. Well-known and respected

16. Called the universal medicine

18. Hot peppers

19. What you have when your head hurts

DOWN

1. The opposite of *mild*

3. Animals that produce chemicals that could be used in making human medicines

4. Toxins

6. Getting well after an illness

10. A colorless and odorless oil found in a plant

12. Something you listen to that can make you feel better

13. Something you take to make you feel better when you are sick

15. A word that means "in a row"

17. One of the most popular drinks in the world

Matthew Savage, Jazz Pianist

In Chapter 2, you read about the healing power of music. This video reports on a nine-year-old boy, Matthew Savage, who is an amazing jazz pianist. He has a disorder called autism, which can cause a person to be emotionally disconnected from others or fixated on routines. As you will see, Matthew's music brings him great happiness and entertains all who listen. Why do you think Matthew became interested in the piano? How do you think playing music may have changed his life?

A Study these words. Then watch the video.

accompanied	inimitable	sensitivity
fixated	innovative	veterans
genius	obsessions	wanders
improvise	profound	wellspring

B All of the statements below are false. Read the statements and then watch the video again. Rewrite each statement to make it true. Add a detail from the video if you can.

1. Matthew Savage usually performs at night.
   Matthew Savage usually performs during the day because he is only nine years old.

2. Matthew's piano talent is especially amazing because he memorizes notes well and plays the jazz greats exactly as they are written.

   _____

   _____

   _____

3. Matthew's parents don't believe that his ability to play the piano is related to his autism.

   _____

   _____

   _____

4. Matthew never earns money for his performances because he is too young.

   _____

   _____

   _____

5. Although Matthew can play the jazz classics very well, he lacks an adult sensitivity, something that will come with age and maturity.

   _____

   _____

   _____

C Discuss these questions with a partner or in a small group.

1. Imagine that you are an adult Matthew Savage looking back on your childhood. Explain how playing music helped you and what role it had in shaping your life.
2. It was fortunate that Matthew's parents introduced him to the piano. How do you think more children with developmental disorders could be exposed to music as a means of coping?

Reader's Journal

Think about the topics and ideas you have read about and discussed in this unit. Pick a topic from the following list, choose one of the discussion questions in the unit, or write about an idea of your own. Write about it for ten to twenty minutes.

- ways music can help heal sick people
- the benefits of garlic, chile peppers, tea, or ginger
- traditional remedies for colds, fevers, or stomachaches in your culture

Vocabulary Self-Test

Complete each sentence with the correct word or phrase.

A
affectionately	hooked up to	remedy
disorders	medicinal	supplemental
enhance	recovering	

1. Some people drink oolong tea for _____ purposes. They think it is a good _____ for stomachaches.

2. The patient was _____ a machine that checks his heart.

3. Salt and pepper can _____ the flavor of food.

4. She _____ calls her daughter "sweetie."

5. Mark is finally _____ after being sick for three weeks.

6. She tries to help people with eating _____.

7. Music is an example of a(n) _____ therapy.

B
adaptation	moderate	straight
beneficial	promotes	well-being
combat	stimulate	

1. Exercise and eating healthy foods can be _____ to your health.

2. She has worked for ten _____ days and is looking forward to her vacation.

3. Most of the students in this class are of _____ ability.

4. Some people use ginger to _____ blood flow.

5. The thick white fur of polar bears is a(n) _____ that helps them survive in the cold.

6. Dr. Lewis _____ using music to help
   _____ depression.

7. Some doctors believe music improves patients' _____
   and shortens their hospital stays.

C defenses   predators   unpalatable
     distinguished   therapeutic   wound
     potent   toxins

1. You should put some medicine on that _____ on your
   arm so it won't get infected.

2. That burned food is _____. I don't want to eat it.

3. Snakes produce _____ in their saliva that can kill
   _____.

4. Dart-poison frogs have developed powerful chemical
   _____ for protection against enemies.

5. Scientists are studying certain species of animals to learn about their
   _____ benefits.

6. This medicine is very _____, so don't take more than
   your doctor prescribes.

7. Dr. Friedman is a(n) _____ heart surgeon. He is
   respected by both his patients and other doctors.

CRIME

Look at the pictures. What do you think the painting and the monkey have in common? They were both stolen. Art theft and the sale of endangered animals are two of the most serious international crimes. In this unit, you will read articles about these crimes and the science of solving crimes.

The Concert *by Vermeer*

Points to Ponder

Think about these questions and discuss them in a small group.

1. Why do you think people would want to steal animals and artwork?
2. Do you watch TV shows about crimes and solving crimes? Which shows?
3. What crimes do you think will decrease in the future? What crimes do you think will increase? Why?

UNIT 6

CHAPTER 1

They're Stealing Our Masterpieces

Art theft is one of the most frequently committed international crimes. Stolen works of art are often very difficult to find, especially when they are well known. Since lawful art collectors and dealers usually refuse to buy them, many stolen works simply disappear into the underground art market. Others are destroyed. Still others are eventually found in unlikely places.

Before You Read

A Discuss these questions with a partner.

1. Have you ever heard of any works of art that were stolen? Which ones?
2. Do you think it would be difficult for someone to steal a painting from a museum in your country? Why or why not?
3. What do you think the punishment should be for art theft?

B Learn the meanings of the following words and phrase before you read the article.

pulled off (1)	legitimate (4)	convicted (7)
ransom (2)	guilty (6)	evidence (10)
obscure (4)	confessed (7)	penalties (18)

They're Stealing Our Masterpieces

by Ira Chinoy

1   In 1990, thieves dressed as police officers snuck into Boston's Isabella Stewart Gardner Museum and pulled off the biggest art theft in history. During the early-morning heist[1], the thieves stole 13 art treasures valued at $200 million or more. Among them were *The Concert*, one of more than 30 paintings by the seventeenth-century Dutch master Jan Vermeer, and Rembrandt's *Storm on the Sea of Galilee*, his only known seascape.

2   Considering how risky it is to sell or hold for ransom a major work of art, the number of important pieces stolen is astonishing. Interpol, the international organization of police, knows of at least 39 works of Rembrandt stolen since 1981. Even more astonishing is that many masterpieces that are too hot[2] to sell and too dangerous to show have never reappeared.

3   Huntington Block, a leading art insurer, says the recovery rate for important works is about 50 percent. That's better than the 10 percent recovery rate for lesser-known works of art. But it still leaves a lot of masterpieces unaccounted for.

4   The more famous the work of art, the more dangerous it is to sell. The goal of most thieves is to steal something valuable enough to be worth their while but obscure enough to sell in the legitimate art market.

5   "If it were known how many legitimate collectors, dealers, and museums have dealt unknowingly in stolen art, there would be a lot of shaking of heads[3]," says Milton Esterow, editor of the magazine *ARTnews*.

6   In some cases, the thieves have held the art for ransom. In October 1989, two thieves stole three van Gogh paintings worth $100 million, in the biggest art theft ever in the Netherlands. The thieves tried to ransom the paintings for $2.5 million but were caught and found guilty. Both were sentenced to prison for three and a half and five years, respectively.

7   One of the strangest cases of art theft is described in *The Art Stealers*, a book by Esterow. In 1961, a visitor to London's National Gallery hid in the museum when it closed for the night. When he thought it was safe, the thief snuck out through a bathroom window with Goya's painting *The Duke of Wellington*. In his ransom demand, the thief asked for money not for himself but for charity. Over the next three and a half years, he made similar demands, but the ransom was never paid. Finally, nearly four years after the painting was stolen, the thief left it, without the frame, at a railway baggage office. A 61-year-old taxi driver later confessed to the crime. He was convicted of stealing the frame but cleared of stealing the painting and got three months in jail.

8   While the Goya painting was missing, several theories about who was responsible for the theft became popular. One theory was that someone had paid criminals to steal the

---

[1] **heist** – a theft

[2] **hot** – likely to cause trouble (slang)

[3] **shaking of heads** – an indication of disbelief

painting for his personal collection. This theory became known as the *Dr. No* theory, after an evil character (Dr. No) in the 1962 James Bond movie *Dr. No*. In the movie, Bond spots the missing Goya painting hanging on one of Dr. No's walls.

9 The so-called stolen-to-order theory has been debated ever since, as one spectacular art theft after another leaves art experts and police puzzled over the fate of so much missing world-class art.

10 Many experts say there's little real evidence that missing masterpieces are hanging on the walls of real-life criminals. But others disagree. FBI agent James D. Keith, who has worked cases in Florida and Texas, believes that some masterpieces are in the hands of drug dealers. "Money is nothing to them," says Keith. "But they like to have things that nobody else has."

11 There are less exotic theories to explain why a lot of fine art just disappears. "Many times the thief doesn't realize that art, unlike jewelry and other commodities, cannot be easily sold," says Los Angeles police detective William E. Martin, one of three police officers in the country investigating art theft full time. "He can't sell it, so he may throw it in his basement or destroy it because he doesn't want to get caught with the evidence."

12 There was just such a case in 1988 in Huntington, New York. Manet's painting *Bouquet of Peonies*, valued at $5 million, was stolen from the Heckscher Museum. Three days later, the thief called the police. He claimed he had taken the painting on impulse and then realized that he would never be able to sell it. He told police they could recover the painting in the laundry room of a New York City apartment building. The police searched but couldn't find the missing Manet painting.

13 Two workmen had already found the painting wrapped in a blanket in the laundry room. Later, the building superintendent

Storm on the Sea of Galilee by Rembrandt, stolen March 1990

thought about hanging the painting in his apartment but decided to leave it in a storage room. The police eventually located the missing work and described the superintendent as "a little shocked" when he found out what he had.

14 Then there was the case of a $50,000 Colonial American painting that surfaced in 1984—on sale for $90 at a church antique show in Lynn, Massachusetts. The painting had been stolen two years earlier in Boston. The antique dealer who put it up for sale told police her son had bought it for $25 from a man selling paintings from the trunk of his car.

15 Milton Esterow tells of a Raphael painting that was stolen from a church in Rome. It was lost or discarded by the thief and then found by an Italian farmer. Years later, the painting was discovered being used to cover a broken window. Stories like this give hope that if important stolen works are not destroyed, they will show up sooner or later—and often where you would least expect them.

16 Sadly, art theft is on the rise. Many high-profile pieces have been stolen in the last five years. One missing painting is Leonardo da Vinci's *Madonna of the Yarnwinder*, which was stolen from Scotland's Drumlanrig Castle in 2003. Another is Edvard Munch's *The Scream*, taken from the Munch Museum in Oslo, Norway, in 2004. Benvenuto Cellini's *Salt Cellar*, a rare gold-plated statue, was stolen from Vienna's Kunsthistorisches Museum in 2003. Fortunately, they have both been recovered. Cellini's *Salt Cellar* was on the FBI's top-ten art crimes list.

17 Thomas Galbraith is the art historian at the Art Loss Register, a company that aids in the recovery of lost or stolen art. He reports that there were 12 significant thefts of valuable art reported in the United States and the United Kingdom in January of 2006 alone. Almost 10,000 art thefts take place around the world every year. Interpol ranks art thefts third among property crimes worldwide and estimates they cost $6 billion a year.

18 Anne Hawley, director of the Gardner Museum, believes that current punishment for art thefts is too mild. "We would like to see stiff[4] penalties for stealing national treasures," she says. "These belong to civilization."

19 Art theft has indeed become a big business.

[4] **stiff** – severe

After You Read

Comprehension Check

A Read these statements. If a statement is true according to the article, write *T* on the line. If it is false, write *F*.

___T___ 1. Many stolen masterpieces seem to disappear.

___F___ 2. It is more dangerous to sell famous works of art than to sell unknown works.

___T___ 3. The goal of most art thieves is to steal the most valuable and well-known work possible.

___T___ 4. Only a few legitimate art dealers have ever bought stolen art.

___F___ 5. Because of the strict punishment for art theft, there are fewer cases of stolen art than ever before.

___T___ 6. Important stolen works often show up in strange places.

___F___ 7. Manet's painting *Bouquet of Peonies* is still missing.

___F___ 8. Like jewelry and other commodities, art can be easily sold.

B The article discusses the opinions of several people involved in the recovery of stolen works of art. Complete the chart by writing the person's name next to his or her opinion.

Name	Opinion
1. Milton Esterow	The number of legitimate collectors, dealers, and museums who unknowingly deal in stolen art is surprising.
2. Hungtington Block	The recovery rate for important works of art is 50 percent.
3. William E. Martin	Many art thieves don't realize how difficult it is to sell stolen art.
4. James D. Keith	Some masterpieces are being held by drug dealers.
5. Anne Hawley	The punishment for art theft is too mild.

✓ **Scanning for Information**

C Scan the article for the answer to each question. Work as quickly as possible.

1. When was Edvard Munch's *The Scream* stolen?
   _2004_

2. Approximately how many art thefts take place around the world every year? _10,000_

3. Who wrote *The Art Stealers*? _Heckscher Museum_

4. When was Manet's painting *Bouquet of Peonies* stolen?
   _1988_

5. What movie shows Goya's painting *The Duke of Wellington*?
   _Dr. No_

F Y I

Picasso is the most popular artist among thieves; 551 of Picasso's works of art have been stolen. Renoir, Rembrandt, and van Gogh are also popular. There have been 209 Renoirs, 174 Rembrandts, and 43 van Goghs stolen.

Vocabulary Practice

A Complete the paragraphs with the words and phrase from the list. Use each word or phrase only once.

2 confessed	3 guilty	9 penalties
4 convicted	7 legitimate	5 pulled off
6 evidence	8 obscure	1 ransom

Edvard Munch's *The Scream* is one of the most famous paintings in the world. Munch painted four versions of the painting, and versions of it have been stolen twice. The first theft occurred in 1994, when two men took less than one minute to climb a ladder, break a window of the National Art Museum in Oslo, Norway, enter the museum, and cut the painting from the wall with wire cutters. The theft took place on the very day that the Winter Olympics began in Norway. The thieves held the painting for _____ransom_____ and demanded $1 million from the government. It was never paid, but several months later, the police found the painting and arrested the thieves. Both of the men __confessed__ to the theft and admitted they were ___guilty___. They were ___convicted___ of robbery and sentenced to prison.

Ten years later, another version of *The Scream* was stolen from the Munch Museum, also in Oslo. This time, two thieves wearing ski masks pulled *The Scream* and another painting, *Madonna*, right off the wall as stunned museum visitors and employees watched helplessly. One of them threatened a staff member with a gun before the pair escaped into a waiting car. In a matter of minutes, the robbers had ___pulled off___ one of the biggest art thefts in recent history. Soon after the theft, the get-away car was recovered and police discovered some important __evidence__. They found parts of the frames of the paintings. Fortunately, *The Scream* was recovered in August of 2006. *Madonna*, however, has never been recovered. Most people believe that it would be impossible to sell it in the __legitimate__ art market because it is so famous. It's one thing to sell an __obscure__ painting but quite another to sell a famous one. Most people agree that we need stiffer __penalties__ for the crime of art theft.

B Cross out the word or phrase in each group that does not belong.

1. famous   well-known   ~~obscure~~   recognized

2. penalty   punishment   consequence   ~~prize~~

3. legal   ~~unlawful~~   legitimate   lawful

4. pulled off   succeeded   ~~failed~~   accomplished

5. ransom   money   payment   painting

6. admit   deny   confess   acknowledge

7. convicted   found guilty   condemned   approved

8. evidence   question   proof   confirmation

SKILL FOR SUCCESS

Learning Two-Word Verbs with *Pull*

In this chapter, you learned that *pull off* means "to accomplish something despite difficulties." Expressions like *pull off* are very common in English. They are called **two-word verbs** because they include a verb and one or more particles (prepositions or adverbs). When these words are used together, they mean something different from what they mean when they are used separately.

C There are many two-word verbs that begin with the verb *pull*. Study the two-word verbs below and complete the sentences that follow. Be sure to use the correct form of the verbs.

- *Pull over* means "to drive a car to the side of the road in order to stop."
- *Pull through* means "to recover from a serious illness or period of difficulties."
- *Pull together* means "to cooperate and work as a group in order to achieve something."
- *Pull for* means "to encourage a person or team to succeed."
- *Pull out* means "to stop being involved in an activity or agreement."

1. After the hurricane, everyone in the city _____ to help each other,

2. At the last minute, the company decided to _____ of the deal.

3. The police officer told us to _____ because we were speeding.

4. John's surgery was long and difficult, but the doctors assured us that he would _____.

5. Good luck, Joey. We're _____ you.

Discuss these questions as a class.

1. Do you agree with Anne Hawley that the punishment for art theft is too mild? What do you think a fair punishment would be?
2. Is art theft taken seriously in your country? Why or why not? Do you know what the punishment is?
3. Do you think that it is right or wrong for museums to offer rewards for the recovery of stolen works? What kinds of problems can this lead to?
4. Many museums are now returning works of art to the country of their origin. Do you agree or disagree that this is a good idea?

UNIT 6

CHAPTER **2**

Crime Lab

Before You Read

A Discuss these questions with a partner.

1. Forensics is a field that uses scientific methods to solve crimes. Are you interested in forensics? Would you like to be a forensic scientist? Why or why not?
2. What techniques do you know of that the police and other crime experts use to solve crimes?
3. Do you think movies and TV shows about crime and police investigations are realistic? Why or why not?

✓ **Previewing and Predicting**

B Preview the article and skim it one time. Then check (✔) the topics that you think will be discussed in the article.

  ❑ 1. Historical information about forensics
  ❑ 2. Appropriate punishment for crimes
  ❑ 3. What forensic scientists do
  ❑ 4. Types of evidence
  ❑ 5. The most notorious criminals in history
  ❑ 6. Inventions in the field of forensics
  ❑ 7. How to commit a crime without getting caught
  ❑ 8. The different kinds of forensic scientists

C Learn the meanings of the following words and phrases before you read the article.

witnesses (1)	astute (8)	disasters (11)
getting away with (4)	wear and tear (11)	monotonous (14)
makes or breaks (7)		

Underlining Important Information

Underlining important information in a passage is another way to help you understand and remember what you read. Read a small section of the material (several paragraphs), think about it, and then underline the information you think is important. Read the next few paragraphs and do the same thing. Continue reading and underlining important information for the rest of the article.

Now read the article carefully and underline the information in the article you think is important. You will use the information you underline to help you answer questions about the article.

Crime Lab

by Emily Sohn

1 Suppose you've just been in a car accident. A sport-utility vehicle hit your little car at high speed. After the accident, your car spun around before crashing into a telephone pole. Luckily, no one was seriously hurt, but the SUV sped away before you had a chance to see its license plate. What do you do? You would probably wait for an ambulance[1] to take you to the hospital to get checked out. Meanwhile, police officers arrived at the scene. They talked to witnesses, examined skid marks, made measurements, took photographs, and collected pieces of glass and other scraps. Then a team of forensic scientists would analyze the data for clues that could lead them to the vehicle (and driver) that hit your car.

2 You may have heard of, or even seen, TV shows such as *CSI: Crime Scene Investigation*. This program and others like it have sparked widespread interest in the tricks and techniques that scientists use to solve legal puzzles.

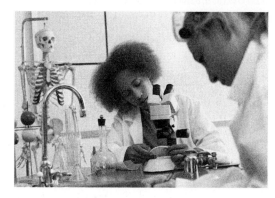

Analyzing skulls and other bones can provide important clues.

What Is Forensics?

3 Forensics is the application of science to solving crimes, and scientists are getting really good at it. "There's no such thing as getting away without a trace," says Jose Almirall. "There's always evidence left behind." Almirall is an analytical chemist and associate director of the International Forensic Research Institute at Florida International University in Miami.

---

[1] **ambulance** – a special vehicle for taking sick or injured people to the hospital

4   Forensic biologists analyze blood, hair, and saliva to identify criminals. Forensic chemists look at powders and other materials for traces of drugs or explosives. Forensic anthropologists study bones to estimate how old people were when they died. There are even forensic meteorologists who track weather patterns. "The field is constantly changing," Almirall says. "That's why research is important. We're always improving the technologies." These new methods and technologies mean that getting away with a crime is becoming harder and harder to do.

5   The first recorded reference to forensics comes from a book written in China in 1248. The book, called *Hsi Duan Yu* (which means *The Washing Away of Wrongs*), explained how to tell the difference between a person who has drowned and a person who has been strangled[2].

6   By the mid-1800s, chemists could identify poisons inside a person's body. In 1892, Englishman Francis Galton provided the first scientific evidence that everyone's fingerprints are unique and could be used as evidence. Now, fingerprints are one of the first things detectives look for at the scene of a crime.

7   Whenever a researcher in any field develops a new technique, forensic scientists look for ways to apply it in their own work. For example, every cell in a person's skin, blood, saliva, or other body part contains a molecule[3] called DNA. No two people (except identical twins) have the same DNA. In the 1980s, biologists figured out how to use DNA as a sort of molecular fingerprint. Since then, DNA testing has become the factor that often makes or breaks a case.

8   Technology alone won't solve a mystery, however. Forensic scientists also have to be astute and recognize that any object is a possible clue. Evidence can include saliva left on a chewed pencil or the back of a stamp. A dog's saliva can prove that the dog bit someone. DNA in wood can be traced back to a tree that was illegally cut from a protected forest. Hair has DNA. So do skin cells that flake off our bodies all the time.

9   "We have a special vacuum cleaner that concentrates such evidence onto a pad," says Almirall. "We can look on the pad for cells." Anyone who's been in a room leaves such traces without knowing it.

10   Piecing clues together to solve puzzles is the fun part of forensics, Almirall says. Visiting crime scenes is tougher. "It's not as glamorous as you might think," he says. "On TV, they make it look cool. But that's a very unpleasant experience for me."

11   Analyzing bones can provide clues about how someone died—and about how a person lived before death. That's the job of forensic anthropologists like Richard Jantz. In his lab, Jantz measures bones and skulls, takes three-dimensional[4] images, and analyzes wear and tear to learn things about bones. Such information provides clues about how old people were when they died and the kinds of things they did when they were alive. Jantz can also tell what people ate and sometimes where they lived, based on chemical analyses of their skeletons. This kind of information is useful when scientists uncover bones in mass graves[5] or find ancient fossils[6]. It also helps

---

[2] **strangle** – to kill someone by pressing his or her throat so that air cannot pass through

[3] **molecule** – the smallest unit into which any substance can be divided without losing its own chemical nature

[4] **three-dimensional** – having length, depth, and height

[5] **mass grave** – a place where several dead bodies have been buried

[6] **fossil** – a part of an animal or plant that lived long ago, or its shape, that is now preserved in rock

them understand disasters, such as plane crashes, and historical mysteries, such as the 1937 disappearance of aviator Amelia Earhart. "Forensic anthropology has grown dramatically in the past 20 years," Jantz says. Jantz's bone collection is an important resource.

The Wide Field of Forensics

12   Forensics is about more than bones and blood. It also helps keep us safe. If you've ever been to an airport, you may have seen an official wipe your luggage with a cloth, put it in a machine, and then have you walk through a metal archway. Forensic chemists invented the machine to catch people who are carrying explosives. It works by using air puffs to dislodge[7] any particles[8] attached to you. Then it analyzes these particles for dangerous substances.

13   Another recent invention uses a special kind of software to match a document with the printer that printed it. The inventors, from Purdue University in West Lafayette, Indiana, are working with U.S. Secret Service agents to apply their new technique. They hope it will help them find the sources of items such as counterfeit[9] money and fake airline boarding passes. This could help them catch terrorists and other criminals.

14   The field of forensics is so broad, Almirall says, that learning it takes a long time. You normally need degrees in more than one science, along with medical knowledge. Then you need to learn how to apply that information at crime scenes. When you're done with all the studying, though, you'll be a different sort of scientist. You'll often find yourself in strange situations, at crime scenes or in front of juries. You'll interact with lawyers, judges, investigators, and scientists with all sorts of specialties. "A typical analytical chemist doesn't do these kinds of things," Almirall says. "Anything can come into the lab as evidence. You don't know what to expect. It's not monotonous."

15   In the end, you might help put dangerous criminals in jail. You might solve mysteries that have been around for decades. You might even save lives or bring peace to families who have lost a loved one. These are things that not every scientist has the opportunity to do. ■

---

[7] **dislodge** – to force something out of position

[8] **particle** – a very small piece of something

[9] **counterfeit** – fake; made as a copy of something else in order to fool people

After You Read

Comprehension Check

A   Read these statements. If a statement is true according to the article, write *T* on the line. If it is false, write *F*.

_____ 1. Most criminals get away without leaving any evidence behind.

_____ 2. The field of forensics is constantly changing.

_____ 3. Every cell in a person's body contains DNA.

_____ 4. Forensics helps keep people safe.

_____ 5. It's easy to become a forensic scientist.

_____ 6. Getting away with a crime is becoming harder.

_____ 7. Solving many criminal cases depends on DNA testing.

B **Answer these questions. Use the information you underlined in the article to help you.**

1. What are two recent inventions that forensic scientists use in their work?

_____

_____

2. What did the Chinese book *Hsi Duan Yu* explain?

_____

3. What information can forensic scientists learn from studying bones?

_____

4. According to the author, what are three things a forensic scientist might do?

_____

_____

_____

Vocabulary Practice

A **Match each word or phrase with the correct definition.**

Word or Phrase	Definition
_____ 1. wear and tear	a. boring because of lack of change
_____ 2. astute	b. someone who saw or heard something related to a crime
_____ 3. make or break	
_____ 4. monotonous	c. damage caused by using something over a period of time
_____ 5. witness	d. to avoid punishment for something
_____ 6. get away with	e. resulting in great success or complete failure
_____ 7. disaster	f. an event that causes harm, damage, or death
	g. clever and intelligent; having good judgment

B Ask and answer these questions with a partner.

1. Who is the most <u>astute</u> person you know? Why do you think he or she is so astute?
2. What kinds of things cause <u>wear and tear</u> on a car?
3. What is the biggest <u>disaster</u> you have read or heard about in the news lately?
4. Have you ever been a <u>witness</u> to a crime?
5. What kinds of things do you find <u>monotonous</u> to do?
6. Do you know anyone who has ever <u>gotten away with</u> cheating on a test? How?

SKILL FOR SUCCESS

Understanding Word Parts: The Suffix -*ist*
The **suffix** *-ist* means "someone who." For example, a *pianist* is someone who plays the piano.

C Write a definition for each term using information from the article.

1. forensic biologists _____

2. forensic chemists _____

3. forensic anthropologists _____

4. forensic meteorologists _____

Talk It Over

Discuss these questions as a class.

1. What personality traits do you think a good forensic scientist needs?
2. How do you think detectives solved crimes 100 years ago? What tools did they have available back then?
3. DNA testing has changed the field of forensic science. What are the advantages of DNA testing? Are there any disadvantages?

UNIT 6

CHAPTER **3**

For Sale: Stolen Animals

Before You Read

 Using Background Knowledge

A Think about what you know about the illegal sale of rare animals. Read the statements in the chart below. Do you agree or disagree with these statements? Check (✔) your response in the *Before You Read* columns. You will check the last two columns after you read the article.

Before You Read		Statements	After You Read	
AGREE	DISAGREE		AGREE	DISAGREE
		1. Every year millions of rare animals are stolen.		
		2. The buying and selling of rare animals is a big business.		
		3. The buying and selling of rare animals causes a serious environmental problem.		
		4. Only a few countries are trying to stop the illegal sale of rare animals.		
		5. Some rare animals sell for thousands of dollars apiece.		
		6. Most pet stores sell stolen animals.		
		7. Many people are fascinated by rare and unusual animals.		

B Learn the meanings of the following words and phrases before you read the article.

smuggle (2)   on the brink of (4)   concealed (8)

cracking down on (4)   tracking down (4)   dreadful (9)

trafficking (4)   poachers (5)

FOR SALE: STOLEN ANIMALS

The Demand for Rare Pets Causes a Crisis for Endangered Species

1   Bright green parrots are jammed[1] into their cages at Mexico City's Sonora Market. Brown snakes lie in a slithery tangle. Toucans[2] squawk loudly as if in protest. It is no wonder they seem unhappy. The animals were stolen from their homes in the wild. Some are rare breeds, which are against the law to sell. Inspectors once found 106 endangered species at the market in a single day.

2   Markets like this one are found all over the world. In Brazil, scarlet macaws stolen from the Amazon rain forest go for $200. In Malaysia, rare blood python snakes are sold for $40. Many buyers smuggle them overseas, where they sell at much, much higher prices.

3   The world's illegal animal trade is worth *problem* several billion dollars a year. Americans buy the most animals, followed by Europeans and Japanese. The trade includes not only live animals but also parts of rare animals, such as rhinoceros[3] horns and tiger bones. These are used in some countries as medicines.

Cracking Down on Crime

4   Cracking down on crimes that involve trafficking in the sale of rare animals has become a high priority. For example, a few years ago, authorities in Mexico arrested Keng Liang Wong, head of a major group of illegal reptile[4] traders. Wong and his group illegally imported and sold more than 300 protected reptiles native to Asia and Africa. Several of the species involved in the illegal trade are on the brink of extinction. *effect #1* Among the animals he was accused of smuggling were Indonesia's rare Komodo dragon and Madagascar's plowshare tortoise. Each sells for up to $30,000! The United States Fish and

Scarlet macaws stolen from the Amazon rain forest sell for $200.

---

[1] **jammed** – pushed with force into a small space

[2] **toucan** – a tropical bird with colorful feathers and a large beak

[3] **rhinoceros** – a very large animal with thick, rough skin and one or two horns on its nose

[4] **reptile** – an animal such as a snake, lizard, or crocodile that lays eggs and uses the heat of the sun to warm its blood

Wildlife Service (FWS) spent several years tracking down Wong, and he finally admitted that he was guilty. Wong was sentenced to 71 months in prison and given a fine of $60,000. "Stealing the world's natural treasures takes a toll that cannot be measured," says Jamie Rappaport Clark, head of the FWS. "It robs countries of their natural heritage, disrupts ecosystems[5], and shortchanges[6] future generations."

Komodo dragon

5   Clark's agency is getting creative in its attempts to catch smugglers. Several years ago, an agent dressed up as an ape and successfully caught a smuggler. Recently, the FWS caught several groups of reptile and bird dealers. Other countries are also working harder at catching and punishing poachers, traders, and smugglers. But it's a difficult job because these thieves keep learning new tricks. Once a rare animal is in a pet store, it's hard to track down its smuggler.

A Brutal Business

6   People have always been fascinated by rare animals. But these days, having one as a pet is considered cool. "People collect rare pets like anything else—stamps, art, cars," says Craig Hoover. He works for an organization called TRAFFIC that watches over illegal trade in wild animals.

7   Rare animals are usually trapped by poor villagers known as poachers. People in Costa Rica, for example, steal newly hatched toucans from their nests. Dealers pay a few dollars to the poacher and then find people to smuggle the animals overseas. "The rarer the species, the higher the price the animal fetches abroad," says Guy Richardson, director in Africa of the World Society for the Protection of Animals.

8   Smugglers use many tricks to sneak animals through airports. They hide live birds in tennis-ball cans and snakes in film containers. Some smugglers tape live lizards to their chests. One smuggler concealed live marmosets (small monkeys) by stuffing them into his pockets!

9   For every smuggled pet sold, several may have died during the rough journey. Wildlife inspectors in Bangkok, Thailand, once found six baby orangutans wedged into crates. Said a Thai wildlife expert, "We had never seen animals in such dreadful conditions."

Where the Wild Things Belong

10   Smuggling not only hurts precious creatures, it also hurts the habitats they leave behind. In an ecosystem, animals depend on one another to maintain a healthy balance. For example, if all white-nosed monkeys disappeared from an area in Africa, then leopards would need to find something else to prey on, and plants that the monkeys eat would grow out of control.

11   Many pet stores promise not to sell stolen animals. "We don't sell anything illegal here," says Kevin Stoltz of New York City's Village Rainforest. "We'd get in big trouble." But some shops keep rare animals hidden in a back room. Others may not know they are selling stolen animals.

---

[5] **ecosystem** – all the living things in an area, and the way they affect one another and their environment

[6] **shortchange** – to treat people unfairly by giving them less than they deserve

12 Even when it is perfectly legal to sell a tortoise, monkey, or macaw, experts hate to see such creatures in a cage. "Every shipment I see breaks my heart," says FWS senior agent Jorge Picon. "These animals belong in the wild."   *solution*

After You Read

Comprehension Check

A Circle the correct answer.

1. How much is the world's illegal animal trade worth a year?
   a. less than a billion dollars
   b. $1 million
   c. billions of dollars
   d. $30,000

2. Why is it so difficult to catch poachers, traders, and smugglers?
   a. They keep learning new tricks.
   b. They make a lot of money.
   c. They live in dreadful conditions.
   d. They rob countries of their natural heritage.

3. Where are markets that illegally sell rare animals found?
   a. only in Europe
   b. all over the world
   c. in very few places
   d. only in the United States

4. What tricks are mentioned in the article that smugglers use to sneak animals through airports?
   a. hiding live birds in tennis-ball cans and snakes in film containers
   b. taping live lizards to their chests
   c. concealing live marmosets by stuffing them into pockets
   d. all of the above

5. Why was Keng Liang Wong arrested?
   a. for cracking down on the crimes
   b. for illegally importing and selling protected reptiles
   c. for dressing up as an ape
   d. none of the above

6. Why does the author use the example of all white-nosed monkeys disappearing from an area in Africa?
   a. to show that white-nosed monkeys sell for a lot of money
   b. to explain how poachers capture the monkeys
   c. to describe how the Fish and Wildlife Service operates
   d. to explain how smuggling animals affects their ecosystems

✓ **Scanning for Information**

B Scan the article for the answer to each question. Work as quickly as possible.

1. Who is the head of the United States Fish and Wildlife Service?
   Jamie Rappaport Clark

2. How much do rare blood python snakes sell for in Malaysia?
   $40

3. How long was Wong's prison sentence?
   71 months

4. What organization does Craig Hoover work for?
   TRAFFIC

5. The parts of what animals are used in some countries as medicines? _____

6. Who is the director of the World Society for the Protection of Animals in Africa? *Guy Kircharch Richardson*

✓ **Summarizing**

C Complete the summary with information from the article.

The selling of rare and endangered animals is an international crime. It's also a big business. The world's *illegal animal trade* (*trafficking*) is
1.
worth *several billions dollars* a year. Rare animals are usually
2.
trapped by *poachers* who sell them to
3.
dealers . The dealers then find people to
4.
smuggle animals overseas, where they are sold for huge
5.
profits. Some rare animals sell for thousands of dollars. The rarer the animal, the more money it is worth. The United States and other countries are trying hard to *catching & punishing poachers* A few
6.
years ago, Mexican authorities were successful when they caught and
arrested *Keng liang Wong* , the head of a major group of
7.
illegal reptile traders. The smuggling and sale of endangered animals is a problem not only because it *hurts precious creatures* but also
8.
because it *hurts the habitat they leave behinds* .
9.

D Look at the statements in the chart on page 172 again and mark *Agree* or *Disagree* for each one in the *After You Read* columns. Talk to a partner about why any of your new responses differed from the ones made before you read the article.

A Match each word or phrase with the correct definition.

	Word or Phrase		Definition
_c_	**1.** concealed	**a.**	someone who catches and steals animals illegally
_h_	**2.** crack down on		
_b_	**3.** dreadful	**b.**	extremely unpleasant or harmful
_d_	**4.** smuggle	**c.**	hidden
_g_	**5.** trafficking	**d.**	to take things or people to or from a place secretly and often illegally
_a_	**6.** poacher		
_f_	**7.** on the brink of	**e.**	to find a person, animal, or object by searching or following a trail
_e_	**8.** track down		
		f.	likely that something will happen soon
		g.	engaging in illegal trading
		h.	to take stronger action on something illegal

B Complete the paragraph with the words and phrases from Exercise A. Use each word or phrase only once. Be sure to use the correct form of the words.

Stories of people who __trafficking__ (1.) in the illegal sale of animals are not at all uncommon. Unfortunately, many of these animals are __on the brink of__ (2.) extinction. For example, there was the case of four young gorillas that had been stolen by __poacher__ (3.) in Cameroon and then __smuggle__ (4.) to Nigeria, where they were sold for $1 million to a zoo in Taiping, Malaysia. In a successful operation in Brazil, the police __track down__ (5.) and arrested several people for illegal trading in endangered birds. They found over 2,000 birds, including macaws, toucans, and parrots, that were being kept in __dreadful__ (6.) conditions while they waited to be illegally shipped to other countries. All five people were found guilty and sentenced to jail. In another story, customs agents in Tibet seized 1,393 pieces of rare animal hides in one of the largest smuggling cases of rare animal hides since 1949. The catch included many rare animals under protection, including Bengal tigers, leopards, lynx, and otters. The hides were discovered in 50 bags __concealed__ (7.) in a truck on the highway. The governments of all countries must continue to __track down__ (8.) these criminals who trade in rare and endangered animals and put them in jail.

SKILL FOR SUCCESS

Understanding Word Parts: The Prefixes *il-*, *ir-*, *im-*, and *in-*

In this unit, you learned the word *illegal*. The prefixes *il-*, *ir-*, *im-*, and *in-* are used to add the meaning "not," "lacking," or "the opposite of" to adjectives and to words formed from adjectives. Follow these spelling rules:

- Use *il-* before words starting with *l*.
  not legal = illegal

- Use *ir-* before words starting with *r*.
  not responsible = irresponsible

- Use *im-* before words starting with *m* and *p*.
  not possible = impossible
  not modest = immodest

- Use *in-* before any other letter.

C Using the prefixes in the chart, write the opposite of each word in the correct box.

visible   complete   legible   mature
literate   probable   relevant   replaceable

il-	ir-	im-	in-
			invisible

D Write a sentence with each word in Exercise C.

1. _____

2. _____

3. _____

4. _____

5. _____

6. _____

7. _____

8. _____

Take a Survey

Ask four people outside of class to answer the questions in the survey. Bring your completed surveys to class and discuss the results with your classmates.

	What do you think the punishment should be for art theft?	**What do you think the punishment should be for illegal animal sales?**
Name		
Name		
Name		
Name		

Tie It All Together

Discussion

Discuss these questions in a small group.

1. Would you like to be a detective? Are you interested in solving crimes? Why or why not?
2. Do you think it is ever all right to break a law? If so, when?
3. Do you think prison is an effective punishment? Why or why not?
4. Can police officers carry guns in your country? Do you think they should be allowed to carry guns? Why or why not?
5. Do you think capital punishment is a good idea? Do you think it can stop people from committing crimes? Why or why not?

Just for Fun

Work with a partner to answer these trick questions.

1. A Chicago lawyer and his wife went to Switzerland for a vacation. While they were skiing in the Alps, the wife skidded over a precipice and was killed. Back in Chicago, an airline clerk read about the accident and immediately phoned the police. The lawyer was arrested and tried for murder.

   The clerk did not know the lawyer or his wife. Nothing he'd heard or seen made him suspect foul play until he read about the accident in the paper.

   Why did he call the police?

2. Bascom turned off the light in his bedroom and was able to get to bed before the room was dark. His bed is 15 feet from the wall switch.

   How did Bascom do it?

3. How can you throw a ball so that it goes a short distance, comes to a dead stop, reverses its motion, and then goes the opposite way? You are not allowed to bounce it off anything, hit it with anything, or tie anything to it.

4. Why do barbers in Los Angeles prefer cutting the hair of ten fat men to cutting the hair of one skinny man?

Video Activity

Saving the Elephants

In Chapter 3, you read about the illegal trade in endangered animals. In this video, you will hear about the threat to African elephants. Although illegal to buy or sell, the ivory from their tusks is highly prized. Being a park ranger who protects the elephants is as dangerous as being a poacher who kills them. Why do you think someone would risk his or her life to protect an animal species?

A Study these words. Then watch the video.

armed	ivory	sanctioned
guard	majestic	stockpiled
herd	orphanage	threat
invincible	pass off	tusks

B Watch the video again. Then complete these sentences with information from the video.

1. Poachers can outsmart and entrap elephants by _____
   _____.

2. The park rangers' job is to _____
   _____.

3. Poachers usually strike _____
   _____.

4. Daphne Sheldrick runs _____
   _____.

5. As long as there is a sanctioned ivory trade, _____
   _____.

C Discuss these questions with a partner or in a small group.

1. Why do you think people want to buy rare things, such as ivory? How can we stop the demand for endangered species and endangered animal parts?

2. Role-play with a partner: You have a chance to interview a poacher about why he or she kills endangered animals. Think of two or three questions you would like to ask and see how your partner responds. Then switch roles. Here are a few questions to get you started:

   • Is the risk worth the reward?
   • Do you understand the impact of harming an endangered species?

Think about the topics and ideas you have read about and discussed in this unit. Pick a topic from the list, choose one of the discussion questions in the unit, or write about an idea of your own. Write about it for ten to twenty minutes.

- how society can prevent violent crimes
- the buying, selling, and smuggling of rare animals
- art theft
- ways technology has helped scientists become better at solving crimes

Vocabulary Self-Test

Complete each sentence with the correct word or phrase.

A confessed   get away with   obscure

   convicted   guilty   penalty

   evidence   legitimate   witnesses

1. When the police caught the man driving the stolen car, he
   _____ to stealing it from his boss.

2. It is difficult to sell stolen paintings in the _____ art
   market.

3. The _____ for parking in a no-parking spot is a $50
   fine.

4. Have you ever heard of Paul Stevens? He's a(n) _____
   twentieth-century artist. Not many people recognize his paintings.

5. After a short trial, she was _____ of the crime. Several
   _____ saw her do it.

6. Fingerprints are often used as _____ in a trial.

7. The jury found the woman _____ of robbery.

8. He thought he could _____ the crime, but eventually he
   got caught and sent to jail.

B disaster   monotonous   ransom

   dreadful   poachers   smuggled

   make or break   pulled off

1. DNA found at a crime scene can often _____ a case.

2. The abandoned children were found living in _____
   conditions.

3. I just read a story in the paper about two men who
   _____ the biggest art theft in years.

4. _____ continue to steal and kill rare animals even though it is illegal.

5. I left in the middle of the movie because it was so long and _____.

6. The thieves demanded a _____ of $1 million for the painting.

7. The plane crash was a terrible _____. Most of the passengers were hurt or killed.

8. Many rare animals are _____ into the United States every year.

C astute   on the brink of   traffic
concealed   tracking down   wear and tear
crack down on

1. The thief _____ the stolen jewelry in his briefcase.

2. It's time to _____ crime in our neighborhood.

3. The _____ woman made a lot of money in the stock market.

4. The seats on the bus took a lot of _____ over the years. It's time to replace them.

5. Many species of animals are _____ extinction.

6. The police had a hard time _____ the people who stole the paintings.

7. The government wants to stop the illegal _____ in drugs.

THE UNIVERSE AND BEYOND

Science has been described as an endless frontier. This is especially true for space science. In this unit, you will read about some of the new technology of space research and how some of the older technology has been put to new uses.

Reprinted courtesy of Howard Post.

Points to Ponder

Think about these questions and discuss them in a small group.

1. Read the cartoon. Do you think it is funny? Why or why not?
2. Do you like to look at the sky at night? What do you think about when you look at the moon and stars?
3. Astronomy is the scientific study of the universe and of objects that exist naturally in space, such as the moon, sun, planets, and stars. Are you interested in astronomy? Why or why not?

UNIT 7

CHAPTER 1

Valuable By-Products of Space Research

Some of the most exciting, and often unexpected, discoveries to come out of research into space travel are products that we use here on Earth. In "Valuable By-Products of Space Research," you will read about some of the many practical, everyday uses of these space-age products.

Before You Read

A Discuss these questions with a partner.

1. What practical benefits of space research can you think of?
2. Space research is very expensive. Do you think the benefits of space research outweigh its cost? Why or why not?

B Learn the meanings of the following words before you read the article.

specialized (1)	device (2)	resistant (8)
anticipated (1)	durable (3)	optimum (10)
spin-offs (1)	monitor (4)	

As You Read

✓ **Underlining Important Information**

In this article, the authors used examples to support their main ideas. As you read, underline the main ideas and examples. This will help you complete the chart on page 190.

Valuable By-Products of Space Research

by David Dooling and Mitchell R. Sharpe

1   Research that went into developing the highly specialized technology for space travel has resulted in many unexpected practical applications back on Earth. Out of the engineering that produced rocket motors, liquid propellants, spacesuits, and other necessities of space flight came by-products that no one had anticipated. Equipment and procedures designed for astronauts and space flights have been successfully adapted for use in medicine, industry, and the home. These valuable by-products of space research, called spin-offs, have improved the quality of life on Earth in many ways.

New firefighter's suit (similar to astronaut's)

2   Some of the best-known examples of spin-offs from space research are found in hospitals and doctors' offices. One such example is the sight switch, which was originally developed to allow astronauts to control their spacecraft without using their hands. The sight switch is now used by disabled people to operate devices using eye movements. Another spin-off is the voice command device, which was designed to enable astronauts to steer their spacecraft by voice command. This device is now being used to help deaf people learn to speak.

3   Doctors have also benefited from the technology required to make miniature electronic instruments small enough and durable enough for trips into space. From this technology have come hearing aids the size of a small pill and tiny television cameras small enough to be attached to a surgeon's head to give medical students a close-up view of an operation. Dentists and their patients have benefited, too. Invisible braces for straightening teeth evolved from NASA (National Aeronautics and Space Administration) research for strong and durable materials for spacecraft.

4   Biotelemetry, which was developed to monitor the physical signs of astronauts by checking their temperature, brain-wave activity, breathing rate, and heartbeat, offers doctors a new means of monitoring hospital patients. Biosensors attached to the body send data by wire or radio. This information is displayed on computer screens for doctors to analyze.

5   Aerospace scientists in England developed a special bed for astronauts that is now used for burn patients. It enables them to float on a cushion of air. Burns can heal more quickly because they do not rub against the bed.

6   Another valuable spin-off came from a special stretcher developed to remove injured workers from the huge propellant tanks of the Saturn V rocket. The stretcher is now widely employed to remove injured workers from mines, oil-drilling rigs, and boats. The rigid

aluminum[1] device permits someone to be moved through an opening 18 inches in diameter. And much of the portable medical equipment carried on ambulances has its roots in NASA's needs for small, portable equipment in space.

7 Many items developed in space research are now being used in homes, factories, and offices. For example, smoke detectors used in homes evolved from technology originally developed for NASA's first space station, Skylab. Cordless tools were first used by the Apollo astronauts to drill into the moon's surface and collect soil and rock samples to bring back to Earth. Today, cordless screwdrivers, drills, and vacuum cleaners are popular in many homes around the world. Fiberglass materials created for rocket-fuel tanks are used to make very strong and durable storage tanks, railway tank cars, and highway tankers. A magnetic hammer that originally served to eliminate small imperfections in the Saturn V rocket is being adapted for use in the automotive and shipbuilding industries.

8 The experience gained from developing NASA spacesuits has been applied to the process of designing clothing for other uses. Firefighters now wear lighter, less bulky clothing made of special "fireblocking" materials that are more resistant to cracking and burning. The spacers used for ventilation and cushioning in moon boots were adapted for use in athletic shoes that are designed to reduce fatigue and injury. Thermal gloves and boots that keep you warm in the winter were also adapted from space technology. These thermal gloves and boots have tiny heating elements that operate on rechargeable batteries. They were used to keep astronauts warm on Apollo missions to the moon.

9 Even watches and clocks have improved because of technologies originally designed for use in spacecrafts. The quartz timing crystals used in many watches and small clocks were first developed for NASA as a highly accurate, lightweight, and durable timing device for the Apollo spacecraft. The bar codes that are now used by stores and manufacturers to keep track of sales and stock were originally developed for NASA as a way to keep track of millions of spacecraft parts.

10 One of the most valuable contributions of aerospace technology to industry is a management technique called the *systems approach*. With the aid of computers, this technique brings together all the elements of a complex project, including people, money, and materials, to assure that everything is completed at the optimum time. It has been applied to a variety of situations unrelated to space exploration. Among them are cancer research, hospital design, city planning, crime detection, pollution control, building construction, and transportation.

11 These are but a few of the more than 30,000 practical applications of space technology that provide daily benefits here on Earth. These spin-offs can be found in hospitals, offices, schools, and homes around the world. So, the next time you look at your watch, put on your sneakers, or check your smoke detector, think about how much safer and more convenient your life is because of the technology that was designed for astronauts and space flights.

[1] **aluminum** – a silver-white metal that is light and easily bent

After You Read

A Circle the correct answer.

1. The article mainly discusses _____.
   a. devices that enable astronauts to control their spacecraft
   b. the value of the systems approach
   c. practical applications of space research
   d. ways of monitoring patients

2. The authors mention applications in all of the following areas EXCEPT _____.
   a. medicine
   b. industry
   c. the home
   d. the law

Earth gets 100 tons heavier every day because of dust falling from space.

3. The authors use tiny hearing aids and television cameras as examples of _____.
   a. spin-offs in the field of clothing design
   b. applications of space research in medicine
   c. inventions by aerospace scientists in England
   d. devices used to enhance the benefits of the systems approach

4. The word *them* in paragraph 5 refers to _____.
   a. aerospace scientists
   b. astronauts
   c. burn patients
   d. doctors

5. Which is an example of a practical application resulting from research that went into developing spacesuits?
   a. storage tanks
   b. firefighters' clothing
   c. cordless tools
   d. invisible braces

6. Where in the article do the authors mention ways to monitor a patient?
   a. paragraph 2
   b. paragraph 4
   c. paragraph 6
   d. paragraph 8

7. With what topic is paragraph 10 mainly concerned?
   a. the importance of management techniques
   b. the complexity of hospital design
   c. uses of computers in industry
   d. applications of the systems approach

8. Bar codes were first developed _____.
   a. as a way to record patients' temperatures
   b. to keep track of sales and stock
   c. to keep track of millions of spacecraft parts
   d. as timing devices for the Apollo spacecraft

B Choose five other spin-offs from the article that you think are valuable. List them in the first column of the chart and complete the other columns with information from the article. Use the information you underlined to help you. Then compare answers with a partner.

Device / Procedure	Space Use / Description	Practical Application
1. *Sight switch*	*lets astronauts control their spacecraft without using their hands*	*permits handicapped people to operate devices using only eye movements*
2.		
3.		
4.		
5.		
6.		

A Match each word with the correct definition.

	Word		Definition
d	1. spin-off	a.	to imagine or expect that something will happen
h e	2. specialized		
c g	3. device	b.	not harmed or affected by something
e	4. durable	c.	an object that has been invented to fulfill a particular purpose
a	5. anticipate	d.	a product that develops from another product
g h	6. monitor		
b	7. resistant	e.	able to last a long time without becoming damaged
f	8. optimum	f.	the best out of a number of possible alternatives
		g.	to watch and check the progress of something
		h.	developed for a particular purpose or job

B Circle the correct answer.

1. If you <u>anticipate</u> that you are going to get a raise in your salary, you _____.
   - a. expect to get a raise
   - b. don't plan on getting a raise

2. If the <u>optimum</u> time to travel to Spain is in the summer, you would probably _____.
   - a. avoid Spain in the summer
   - b. plan a trip to Spain in the summer

3. A material that is <u>resistant</u> to water _____.
   - a. keeps water out
   - b. lets water in

4. An example of a <u>spin-off</u> of space technology is a special bed for _____.
   - a. astronauts
   - b. burn patients

5. <u>Durable</u> tires for your car _____.
   - a. need to be replaced very often
   - b. should last for a long time

6. Which is an example of a specialized device? *machine*
   a. an electronic microscope
   b. a book of poetry

7. Which would a nurse be more likely to monitor?
   a. a patient's heart rate
   b. a customer's purchases

✓ **Learning Synonyms and Antonyms**

C For each pair of words, circle *S* if they are synonyms or *A* if they are antonyms.

1. spin-offs	by-products	S	A
2. device	machine	S	A
3. durable	weak	S	A
4. optimum	worst	S	A
5. monitor	check	S	A
6. resistant	vulnerable	S	A
7. adapted	modified	S	A
8. anticipate	predict	S	A

SKILL FOR SUCCESS ✓

Understanding Word Parts: The Suffix -ize
In this chapter, you learned the meaning of the verb *specialize*. It is formed by adding the **suffix -ize** to the adjective *special*. The suffix -ize is used to make verbs from adjectives and nouns. Note: Sometimes the spelling of the verb changes when this suffix is added.

D Add the suffix *-ize* to each noun or adjective to make a verb. Use your dictionary for help with spelling. Then write a sentence using each word.

1. special: ___*specialize*___

   _____

2. memory: _____

   _____

3. symbol: _____

   _____

4. agony: _____

_____

5. final: _____

_____

6. modern: _____

_____

Talk It Over

Discuss these questions as a class.

1. Have you ever used any of the spin-offs mentioned in the article? If so, describe when and why.
2. Do you think any of the spin-offs from space technology are more valuable than their originally intended purpose? Which one(s)?

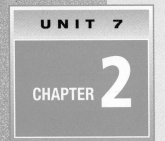
Destination Mars

Before You Read

A Discuss these questions with a partner.

1. Are you interested in space travel? Do you have any desire to travel to another planet? Why or why not?
2. Do you think space exploration is important? What can scientists learn from studying other planets?
3. Do you think there is life anywhere else in the universe? Explain your answer.

✓ **Skimming for the Main Idea**

B Skim the article one time. Circle the correct answer.

1. What is the article mainly about?
   a. the benefits of space research
   b. new research about the planet Mars
   c. the possibility of life on Mars

2. What is the aim of the article?
   a. to get the reader excited about the new research
   b. to dissuade the reader from going to Mars
   c. to teach the reader how to measure gravity on Mars

3. What is the tone of the article?
   a. humorous
   b. depressing
   c. enthusiastic

C Learn the meanings of the following words and phrase before you read the article.

missions (1)	collaborators (6)	boost (11)
iron out (3)	automated (6)	composition (12)
gravity (3)	shelters (9)	

Destination Mars

by Emily Sohn

1 If you're lucky, you might someday walk on the surface of Mars. For some scientists, the question is no longer WHETHER people will ever get to Mars. It's a question of WHEN people will travel there. The most cautious of the bunch say it may take many decades to overcome the obstacles standing in the way of such an expedition. Others are more optimistic. "I'd like to think that missions will be going there as early as 15 years from now," says Paul Wooster. He's director of the Mars Gravity Biosatellite Program at the Massachusetts Institute of Technology (MIT).

2 Whether or not you want to go to Mars yourself, the Red Planet is exciting. Two radio-controlled robots, or rovers, named *Spirit* and *Opportunity*, are now exploring the planet. The rovers are sending back amazing images and information about places that scientists had never before studied in such detail.

3 Before any of us can vacation on Mars, though, there are still plenty of complications to iron out. Some of the biggest questions have to do with the human body. We are fine-tuned[1] to deal with conditions here on Earth. No one knows how our bodies might react to living on another planet. Gravity, in particular, is a big concern. Because Mars is smaller and less massive than Earth, its gravity is weaker than Earth's. A person weighing 100 pounds on Earth would weigh just 38 pounds on Mars. What's more, astronauts would experience zero gravity during the year or more of travel time going to and from Mars.

Radio-controlled robots, named Spirit *and* Opportunity, *are now exploring Mars.*

4 When astronauts spend time in zero gravity, their muscles and bones break down. It's as if they had been lying motionless in bed for a long time. If astronauts don't do weight-bearing exercises while they're in orbit aboard the space shuttle or space station, it can be difficult for them to walk when they get back. The longer astronauts spend in space, the longer it takes them to recover. A mission to Mars would last at least two and a half years, including travel time. That's much longer than anyone has previously spent in outer space.

Mice in Space

5 To find out how mammals might get along on Mars, Wooster is planning to send 15 mice into outer space. Each mouse will have its own cage. For five weeks, the spacecraft will spin just enough for the mice to experience the gravitational pull found on Mars.

---

[1] **fine-tune** – to make small changes in something to make it the best it can be

6   Over the course of the mission, Wooster and his collaborators (which include more than 100 college students around the world) will monitor the health and activity levels of the mice. Each cage will be built to collect urine samples on cloth pads underneath a mesh[2] barrier at the bottom of the cage. Every few days, an automated system will roll up and store the urine-soaked pads. When the mission returns to Earth, the scientists will look at chemical markers in the urine to measure how quickly muscles and bones break down. "This is going to be the longest partial-gravity study on mammals in space," says Wooster, who hopes to launch the mission next year.

7   What happens to mice could also happen to people. The data that researchers collect will help determine how much exercise and what types of activity Mars travelers might need to stay healthy and strong for the entire trip.

8   Travel to Mars presents other complications. Mars doesn't have any grocery stores or fast-food restaurants. Plants don't even grow there. And the rovers still haven't found pools of liquid water on the planet. So, astronauts will have to bring all their food and water with them—enough to last several years.

9   Also, it will be impossible for people to breathe Martian air, which is 95 percent carbon dioxide. Earth's atmosphere is 78 percent nitrogen, 21 percent oxygen, and about 0.035 percent carbon dioxide. Therefore, astronauts will need reliable spacesuits, pressurized[3] vehicles, and airtight[4] shelters to survive on Mars.

10   Heavily insulated clothes will also be essential. Because Mars is farther from the sun than Earth, it gets extremely cold in winter, with temperatures as low as −111 degrees Celsius. And a Martian year lasts 687 Earth days, so that's a lot of cold days.

Planetary Research

11   Putting people on Mars would be a huge boost for planetary research, Wooster says. "In a couple of hours at most, an astronaut can do pretty much everything the rovers there are doing currently," he says. "And an astronaut can do it much better and more comprehensively."

12   Already, *Spirit* and *Opportunity* have turned up some interesting findings about the rocks, dirt, and landscape of Mars. *Opportunity*, for instance, dug a trench with its front wheel. Analyses showed that the soil composition changes with depth. The way the soil is packed together suggests the presence of small amounts of water in the past. On the other side of the planet, *Spirit* found the top layer of soil to be stickier than expected. One possibility is that liquid water that was once present in the soil combined with salts to produce the stickiness.

13   Finding water on Mars would be an enormous triumph. Water makes life possible here on Earth. So, finding signs of water on Mars would indicate that life might have existed there in the past and could still be there today.

14   Today, mobile robots are exploring Mars. In a few years, mice may experience Mars in their own way. Looking farther ahead, people like you might get to walk across the Red Planet's dusty surface one day. ■

---

[2] **mesh** – material made of threads or wires that have been woven together like a net

[3] **pressurized** – refers to an aircraft in which the air pressure inside is similar to the air pressure on the ground

[4] **airtight** – not allowing air to get in or out

After You Read

A Answer these questions with information from the article.

1. Who is Paul Wooster?

   He is director of the Mars Gravity Biosatellite program at the MA .

2. What are *Spirit* and *Opportunity*?

   Two radio-controlled robots that exploring the planet

3. What are they doing?

   They are sending back amazing images & information

4. What problems do scientists have to resolve so that astronauts can survive on Mars?

   weight

5. Why is Wooster sending mice into space?

   to see how mammals might get along on Mars.

6. Why would finding water on Mars be such an important discovery?

   b/c if there's water on Mars, that's means there's life.

F Y I

Mars is named after the Roman god of war. Mars is sometimes referred to as the Red Planet because of its reddish appearance when seen from Earth at night.

✓ Identifying Facts and Opinions

B Decide if each statement is a fact or an opinion. Check (✓) the correct box.

	Fact	Opinion
1. If you're lucky, you might someday walk on the surface of Mars.		✓
2. Earth's atmosphere is 78 percent nitrogen, 21 percent oxygen, and about 0.035 percent carbon dioxide.	✓	
3. When astronauts spend time in zero gravity, their muscles and bones break down.	✓	
4. Finding water on Mars would be an enormous triumph.		✓
5. Whether or not you want to go to Mars yourself, the Red Planet is exciting.	✓	✓
6. A person weighing 100 pounds on Earth would weigh just 38 pounds on Mars.	✓	

A Match each word or phrase with the correct definition.

Word	Definition
_____ **1.** mission	**a.** someone working with others to achieve something
_____ **2.** iron out	
_____ **3.** gravity	**b.** the force that attracts objects toward one another
_____ **4.** collaborator	
_____ **5.** composition	**c.** a special trip made by a spacecraft or military aircraft
_____ **6.** automated	**d.** an improvement or increase in something
_____ **7.** shelter	**e.** something (such as a building or tent) that protects you from the weather
_____ **8.** boost	
	f. to resolve problems by removing difficulties
	g. operated by machines or computers
	h. the parts, substances, etc., that something is made of

B Complete each sentence with the correct word or phrase from Exercise A. Be sure to use the correct form of the words.

1. There is less _____ on the moon than on Earth.

2. We are living in a temporary _____ because our house was destroyed in the hurricane.

3. We _____ a few problems, and now the plan is working well.

4. A _____ to Mars would take about two and a half years.

5. Dr. Johnson and his _____ are developing a new device to measure the blood pressure of astronauts.

6. The new shopping center was a _____ to the economy of our city.

7. When we studied the _____ of the rock, we found it contained quartz.

8. *ATM* stands for _____ *teller machine*.

Understanding Word Parts: The Suffixes -*able* and -*ible*
The suffixes -*able* and -*ible* form adjectives from verbs. For example, *rely* (a verb) becomes *reliable* (an adjective). Note: Sometimes the spelling of the adjective changes when this suffix is added.

C Complete the chart. Add -*able* or -*ible* to each verb to make an adjective. Use your dictionary for help with spelling.

Verb	Adjective
1. achieve	
2. adjust	
3. flex	
4. enjoy	
5. identify	
6. observe	

D Complete each sentence with the correct verb or adjective from Exercise C. Use your dictionary to help you.

1. I hope you'll _____ the show about our solar system.

2. You need to _____ the color on your TV to get a better picture.

3. Stretching exercises will make your body more _____.

4. We plan to _____ the behavior of four types of fish in this pond.

5. Your goals are challenging, but I think they are _____.

6. She is wearing a bright yellow hat, so she will be easily _____ in the crowd.

Talk it Over

Discuss these questions as a class.

1. Would you like to visit Mars in the future? Why or why not?
2. In addition to the physical difficulties of living on Mars, what other problems might astronauts on the planet face?
3. Why do you think Mars is a good place to study to find out whether there is life anywhere else in the universe?

Research a Planet

Use the Internet or library to do some research about one of the planets in our solar system. Use the list below as a guide. Share your information with your classmates.

- name of the planet
- how the planet got its name
- size and diameter of the planet
- description of the planet's rotation around the sun
- moons
- your weight on the planet
- distance from Earth and distance from the sun
- the planet's average temperature

Dancing to the Music of Physics

Many people feel that there is a wall dividing the worlds of art and science and that artists and scientists are very different types of people. Physicist Steve Huber is someone who doesn't fit the stereotype. In this interview, "Dancing to the Music of Physics," Dr. Huber talks about the connection between art and science.

Before You Read

A Discuss these questions with a partner.

1. How would you describe a typical artist? What words would you use to describe an artist?
2. How would you describe a typical scientist? What words would you use to describe a scientist?
3. Do you think that art and science are very different disciplines? How are they different?
4. Can you think of any ways that art and science are similar? Explain the ways.

B Learn the meanings of the following words and phrase before you read the interview.

was into (something) (3)	indefinable (7)	precise (10)
misconception (7)	apparent (8)	rotation (15)
distinction (7)	arbitrary (10)	

Dancing to the Music of Physics

Physics professor Dr. Steve Huber dances to a Vivaldi concerto.

1 Dr. Steve Huber is a physics professor and an accomplished musician. As an undergraduate student, he had two majors—physics and music. Dr. Huber worked his way through graduate school as a rehearsal pianist for several ballet companies. At age 23, he began to study dance, and after several years of training, he performed professionally for a short time with Ballet Elan. Subsequently, he continued as a guest artist for a variety of other ballet companies while completing his Ph.D. in theoretical physics.

2 **When did you first become interested in physics?**

3 I can't remember a time when I wasn't interested in physics. When I was a child, I was very curious about the world around me. For example, I always wondered why light behaves the way it does. I found it more fun to play with a prism[1] than to play with the kids in the neighborhood. I wasn't very social, but I was really into figuring out how things worked. I got my own telescope when I was eight years old, and I loved to take it out at night and go star-gazing. I would look at the planets and stars and wonder what was out there. When I was ten, my father bought me a book on the universe, and I just ate it up[2]. In fact, I still have that book right here in my office.

4 **How about music? When did you become interested in music?**

5 It was the same with music. I've always had a natural ear for music, perfect pitch[3]. Even as a young child, if I heard a song on the radio, I could go right to the piano and play it. When I heard a sound like the ring of a telephone, I could identify its pitch and play the note on the piano. However, I didn't develop a serious interest in becoming a pianist until I was in college. I also seemed to do well in school in the visual arts like painting and drawing.

6 **What similarities do you see between music and physics?**

7 It's not uncommon for physicists to become accomplished musicians. There is a common misconception that art and science are completely separate from each other. I think the distinction is artificial. In reality, art and science are not as mutually exclusive[4] as one might assume. Solving a complicated mathematical problem, for example, can require the same degree of creative thinking

---

[1] **prism** – a transparent block of glass that breaks up white light into different colors

[2] **eat it up** – to enjoy it very much

[3] **perfect pitch** – the ability to identify or sing any musical note

[4] **mutually exclusive** – refers to two things that cannot both exist or be true at the same time

as painting a landscape or writing a poem or piece of music. I feel an indefinable tingle[5] when I play the Schumann concerto or dance to *Romeo and Juliet*. I get that same tingle from theoretical physics.

8 The beauty of art is readily apparent to most people. However, in the case of theoretical physics, the beauty is not nearly as accessible to the general public, but it is every bit as beautiful. Nature seems to follow certain principles, very much the same way that art does.

9 **What is the relationship between music and math?**

10 Music theory is a very mathematical discipline. Relationships among various notes in classical harmony are based on simple mathematical relationships. For example, a note that is a perfect octave[6] above another note is exactly twice the frequency of the original note. It took thousands of years for the musical scales to evolve into the major and minor scales that we have today. The relationship among the various notes in a scale is not arbitrary. What makes the sounds work together in harmony has precise mathematics behind it. For example, there are very good technical reasons why a song may feel finished when it ends on one kind of chord[7], but feel unresolved when it ends on another kind.

11 **You have said that physics is beautiful. What makes it beautiful to you?**

12 To me, it's incredible the way nature seems to work so perfectly. I think it is beautiful. I always tell my students on the first day of class, "If you like reading Sherlock Holmes detective stories, you'll like doing physics problems." Physics is about figuring things out—discovering how they work, just like detective work.

13 A lot of people fear physics because they view it as a big complicated jumble of facts that have to be memorized. But that's not true; it's an understanding of how nature works, how the various parts interact. One can view art and literature as the relationships and interactions of ideas. Likewise, physics studies the relationships and interactions of concepts. In other words, to me art and science fundamentally attempt to achieve the same objective—an understanding of the world around us!

14 The whole universe seems to follow some very basic principles as it evolves in time. Two of these principles are the conservation of energy and the conservation of angular momentum. These conservation laws of physics are like basic checking accounts. You can put money in and take it out, but all the money is accounted for. In the case of energy conservation, you can make energy deposits and energy withdrawals, but all the energy is accounted for.

15 The conservation of angular momentum governs the rotation of objects. This law applies to everything in the universe, including the rotation of stars, the rotation of the planets and their orbits, the behavior of an electron in an atom, the spin of a figure skater, and the rotation of wheels on a truck. What it all comes down to in the end is that everything in the universe fits together like the pieces of a perfect puzzle. As Einstein said, "The most incomprehensible thing about the universe is that it is comprehensible."

---

[5] **tingle** – a physical sensation

[6] **octave** – the space between two musical notes that are eight musical notes apart

[7] **chord** – a combination of three or more musical notes played at the same time

Comprehension Check

A Complete the paragraph with information from the interview. Fill in as many blanks as you can without looking back at the text. You do not have to use the exact words from the interview as long as the idea is correct.

Dr. Steve Huber is ﹏﹏﹏﹏﹏ and ﹏﹏﹏﹏﹏. He believes that
                1.   2.
﹏﹏﹏﹏﹏ and ﹏﹏﹏﹏﹏ are similar. According to Dr. Huber,
   3.   4.
both disciplines require ﹏﹏﹏﹏﹏. He also thinks that everything in
                   5.
﹏﹏﹏﹏﹏ is governed by ﹏﹏﹏﹏﹏.
   6.   7.

✓ **Making Inferences**

B Check (✔) the statements you think Dr. Huber would agree with.

❏ 1. The beauty of physics is more accessible than the beauty of art.
❏ 2. Physics is more exciting than art.
❏ 3. The whole universe is governed by very basic principles.
❏ 4. Music is a very mathematical discipline.
❏ 5. Unlike art, physics attempts to understand the world around us.
❏ 6. Physics should be feared.
❏ 7. Einstein's idea that "The most incomprehensible thing about the universe is that it is comprehensible" is true.

SKILL FOR SUCCESS ✓

Understanding Comparisons

Authors often compare people, events, things, or ideas to show how they are alike. English uses many special words and phrases to show **comparisons**. Look for these signal words and phrases that show similarities:

like	at the same time	in the same way
likewise	in comparison	
similarly	in the same manner	

C List the three similarities between the arts and science that Dr. Huber mentions.

1. ﹏﹏﹏﹏﹏﹏﹏﹏﹏﹏﹏﹏﹏﹏﹏﹏﹏﹏﹏﹏﹏﹏﹏﹏

2. ﹏﹏﹏﹏﹏﹏﹏﹏﹏﹏﹏﹏﹏﹏﹏﹏﹏﹏﹏﹏﹏﹏﹏﹏

3. ﹏﹏﹏﹏﹏﹏﹏﹏﹏﹏﹏﹏﹏﹏﹏﹏﹏﹏﹏﹏﹏﹏﹏﹏

A Circle the correct answer.

1. An <u>arbitrary</u> decision is _____.
   a. planned and based on reason
   b. based on personal feelings, not logic

2. If there is a clear <u>distinction</u> between two languages, they are
   a. almost the same
   b. different

3. If something is <u>apparent</u>, it is _____.
   a. obvious
   b. unclear

4. If you <u>are into</u> doing yoga, you _____.
   a. don't enjoy it
   b. like doing it

5. The <u>rotation</u> of an object refers to its _____.
   a. turning motion
   b. complexity

6. An <u>indefinable</u> concept is _____.
   a. easy to explain in words
   b. difficult to describe

7. A <u>misconception</u> about an idea is _____.
   a. wrong
   b. correct

8. If you need the <u>precise</u> location of a doctor's office, you need the
   _____.
   a. exact address
   b. general location

B Write a sentence with each underlined word or phrase in Exercise A.

1. _____
2. _____
3. _____
4. _____
5. _____
6. _____
7. _____
8. _____

Understanding Word Parts: The Suffix *-ical*

The suffix *-ical* is used to form adjectives from nouns. Note: Sometimes the spelling of the adjective changes when this suffix is added.

C Complete the chart. Add or delete *-ical*. Use your dictionary for help with spelling.

Noun	Adjective
1. mechanics	*mechanical*
2.	grammatical
3. history	
4. mathematics	
5.	geographical
6. medicine	
7. music	
8.	philosophical
9. politics	
10.	theoretical

D Complete each sentence with the correct noun or adjective from Exercise C.

1. A doctor would give you _____ advice.

2. _____ scales are based on _____.

3. The United States has two main _____ parties: the Democratic Party and the Republican Party.

4. A country's mountains, rivers, and lakes are part of its _____.

5. The library has an important collection of our city's _____ documents that explain how the city was founded.

6. This letter has several _____ mistakes. Please check the verb tenses and correct them.

7. My _____ on life is to live each day to the fullest.

8. My car has many _____ problems. I hope the mechanic can fix them.

9. Do you understand the _____ of relativity?

Talk It Over

Discuss these questions as a class.

1. Dr. Huber states that many people fear physics. Is this true for you? Why do you think that so many people are afraid of physics?
2. Do you believe that there is a wall dividing art and science? Are you or is anyone you know interested in both art and science?
3. Have you ever read any Sherlock Holmes mysteries? Do you agree that they are like physics problems? Why or why not?

Learning Academic Abbreviations

A In this interview, you learned that Dr. Huber has a Ph.D. in theoretical physics. *Ph.D.* stands for *Doctor of Philosophy*. A Ph.D. is the highest degree awarded by a graduate school. Study the list below of other academic degrees and their abbreviations.

Academic Degrees

B.A.	Bachelor of Arts
B.S.	Bachelor of Science
D.D.S.	Doctor of Dental Surgery
D.V.M.	Doctor of Veterinary Medicine
J.D.	Doctor of Law
M.A.	Master of Arts
M.B.A.	Master of Business Administration
M.D.	Doctor of Medicine
M.E.	Mechanical Engineer
M.S.	Master of Science

B Use the Internet or library to find out what degrees these abbreviations stand for.

1. E.E. _____

2. D.M.D. _____

3. M.S.W. _____

Discussion

Discuss these questions in a small group.

1. Do you agree with Einstein that the universe is comprehensible? Explain your answer.
2. Do you think time and money should be spent on exploring space, or would they be better spent helping people on Earth?
3. Philosopher Will Durant wrote in 1926, "Every science begins as philosophy and ends as art." Do you agree with this idea? Why or why not?

Just for Fun

Try to solve these toothpick puzzles. You'll need about 15 toothpicks to solve the puzzles.

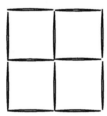

1. Change the positions of four toothpicks to make three small squares, all the same size, with no toothpicks left over.

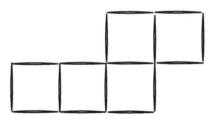

2. Change the positions of two toothpicks to make four small squares, all the same size, with no toothpicks left over.

3. Remove six toothpicks completely, leaving ten on the table.

4. Move the position of one toothpick and make the house face east instead of west.

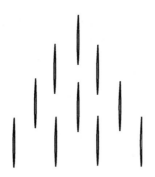

5. Change the positions of three toothpicks so that the triangular pattern points down instead of up.

6. The picture shows how to make four triangles with nine toothpicks. Can you find a way to make four triangles with only six toothpicks? Hint: The solution to this toothpick teaser is different from the solutions to the other five. It will require a completely new approach.

Video Activity

Rocket Men

In this video, you will learn about inventors who are trying to create vehicles to carry ordinary people into space. Have you ever thought about taking a vacation in space? Do you think this is something that will be possible in your lifetime?

A Study these words. Then watch the video.

cargo	frontier	shortage
commercial	jackpot	suborbital
forefront	manned	undaunted

B Read these questions and then watch the video again. Circle the correct answers.

1. Burt Rutan thinks that in 42 years, NASA should have achieved more _____.
   a. manned space flights
   b. moon landings
   c. suborbital flights
2. Private companies are now competing to finance, build, and launch a manned space mission. This would win them the X-prize and be a first step toward _____.
   a. the $10 million jackpot
   b. commercial space travel
   c. space hotels

3. Steve Bennett, a space inventor, foresees a day when private carriers will ship cargo around the solar system and ordinary people will be able to _____.
   a. become astronauts
   b. compete for the X-prize
   c. vacation in space
4. There are _____ inventors who want to go into space and are unafraid of flying in experimental private carriers.
   a. many
   b. few
   c. no

C Discuss these questions with a partner or in a small group.

1. If it were possible to vacation in space, would you go? Is there a particular planet you would like to see or visit?
2. Years ago, certain countries were in a space race: a competition to see how quickly they could land astronauts on the moon. Now there is competition among inventors to create private carriers to transport people and cargo in space. This competition is fueled by a fascination with space as a frontier and a drive to make money in a new industry. Do you think the commercialization of space travel is a good thing? How could it better our world? In what ways could it hurt us?

Reader's Journal

Think about the topics and ideas you have read about and discussed in this unit. Pick a topic from the list, choose one of the discussion questions in the unit, or write about an idea of your own. Write about it for ten to twenty minutes.

- why you would or would not like to travel to another planet
- your ideas about life in other places in the universe
- why governments should or should not spend so much money on space-research programs

Vocabulary Self-Test

Complete each sentence with the correct word or phrase.

A anticipate   boost   monitor
   apparent   device   optimum
   arbitrary   distinction   precise

1. The doctor is going to _____ my cholesterol level.

2. Getting a good grade on the test was a(n) _____ to my confidence.

3. He invented a new _____ for measuring very small distances.

4. I need to know the exact weight, so we are looking for a more _____ method of measurement.

5. The difficulty of the problem was obvious. It was _____ to me right away.

6. Do you know the _____ amount of sun this plant needs?

7. Do you understand the _____ between jazz and blues? Sometimes I can't tell the difference.

8. It's hard to _____ what the weather will be like next month.

9. His decision to sell his share of the business seemed _____. He didn't even discuss it with his partners.

B are into   indefinable   resistant
   collaborators ironed out   specialized
   durable   misconception

1. If you have a(n) _____ feeling, you can't explain it in words.

2. It's a common _____ that money brings happiness.

3. People who _____ cooking like to cook.

4. A(n) _____ product should last a long time.

5. If a material is _____ to fire, it should not burn easily.

6. Once you have _____ all of the problems in the new production process, things should go smoothly.

7. Your _____ on this project will work with you to accomplish your goal.

8. Some of the _____ technology for space travel has been adapted for new purposes.

C automated   mission   shelter
   composition   rotation   spin-offs
   gravity

1. The building was designed to provide a(n) _____ for people who lost their homes during the flood.

2. Scientists are studying the _____ of rocks found on the moon.

3. The force of _____ on Earth is stronger than it is on Mars.

4. Astronauts are taking two dogs with them on their _____ to the moon.

5. We have a(n) _____ production process; machines do all the work.

6. The _____ of Earth takes 24 hours.

7. There have been many useful _____ from the technology developed for the space program.

BUSINESS SAVVY

The world of business is changing more quickly than ever before as both companies and consumers become more savvy. In this unit, you will read about some of the ways that companies are trying to market their products and become successful players in the international economy.

Points to Ponder

Think about these questions and discuss them in a small group.

1. How do you think the way people and companies do business has changed in recent years?
2. Would you like to work in another country? Why or why not?
3. What kinds of challenges do you think companies face today?
4. What kinds of ads do you like? Describe them and give some examples. What kinds of ads do you dislike? Why?

CHAPTER **1**

Nothing but the Truth

Before You Read

A Discuss these questions with a partner.

1. Do you read the labels on products? Does the information on the product label influence your purchasing decisions? How?
2. Do you try to buy products that are safe for the environment? Why or why not?
3. Do you try to eat healthy food? Do you look for products that are supposed to be healthy? Why or why not?
4. When you buy something, how important is each of the following to you? Check (✔) the boxes that are true for you and then compare answers with a partner.

	Very Important	Somewhat Important	Not Important
1. The price			
2. The way it looks			
3. The quality			
4. The brand			
5. Its impact on the environment			
6. Where it was made			
7. How healthy it is			

✓ **Skimming for the Main Idea**

B Skim the article one time. Circle the correct answer.

1. What is the article about?
   a. the threat of global warming and the destruction of the ozone layer
   b. the trend in advertising to market products as healthy and environmentally safe

2. What is the purpose of the article?
   a. to help the reader become a more aware consumer
   b. to persuade the reader to buy environmentally safe products

C Learn the meanings of the following words before you read the article.

poll (3)	boasts (6)	minuscule (11)
genuine (4)	guidelines (7)	forbidden (12)
exaggerated (4)	strict (10)	

Nothing but the Truth

by Sean McCollum

1 For manufacturers and advertisers, the marketing of "ecofriendly" and "healthy, all-natural" products can mean big profits. But how can the consumer tell fact from fancy[1]?

2 Pick an aisle, any aisle, and roll your shopping cart along the supermarket shelves. What words do you see? "Fat free!" "Lite!" "100% Recycled!" "Low Sugar!" "Earth-friendly!" "Heart healthy!" Welcome to the wonderful world of green[2] and health-conscious marketing, one of the biggest trends in consumer advertising.

3 Americans have always expressed their passions and concerns through the products they buy. And recently, no two issues have been of more concern to the American consumer than the environment and health. Because of the many reports about the threat of global warming, the destruction of the ozone layer, how fatty foods damage the heart, and why sugar isn't good for you, shoppers have begun paying closer attention to the products they buy. Poll after opinion poll shows that Americans are eager to buy healthier and environmentally safer products—and pay more for them, if necessary.

---

[1] **fancy** – something that is not real

[2] **green** – friendly to the environment

4   Manufacturers got the message loud and clear, and soon big advertisers jumped on the eco-health bandwagon. But while some companies made genuine improvements in their products to attract the green consumer, others exaggerated their improvements and just added a few catchy[3] words to their packages.

5   Tom's of Maine is one company that's done well with genuinely environmentally sensitive products. Tom's toothpaste boxes, and boxes for other items, are all made with 100 percent recycled paper. Plastic bottles are all made with polyethylene—an easily recyclable plastic. The company also sells refills of its deodorants so customers can reuse the plastic bottles.

6   Most manufacturers don't go to these lengths, though that doesn't stop them from making exaggerated claims about the environmental benefits of their products. Although a box of computer paper may say it's "recycled," it may contain as little as 50 percent wastepaper. A hairspray that boasts it contains "No CFCs"— gases that destroy the earth's ozone layer—may use another ozone-eater, trichloroethane, instead. A shampoo manufacturer may claim its plastic bottle is recyclable, but if it's made of polyvinyl chloride, it's not. Apparently, the attitude of some manufacturers is, "What you don't know won't hurt you."

7   Now, the federal government has started taking a close look at companies making exaggerated environmental claims. The Federal Trade Commission (FTC), the agency charged with protecting consumers from misleading advertising, has issued guidelines on what environmental claims can and can't be made.

8   How can consumers know if a manufacturer is exaggerating the truth? A nonprofit organization called Green Seal helps. Green Seal is an

independent tester of "green" products. It's asking companies to voluntarily submit their goods to Green Seal for testing. If they meet the group's standards, then the companies will be allowed to place the Green Seal logo—a blue globe with a green checkmark—on their packaging.

Cracking Down on Claims

9   Although "green seals" have shown up on shampoo bottles, there isn't a "health seal" to help clear up the confusion about which foods are good for you. With more and more people concerned with eating healthy, more and more food manufacturers are making fanciful claims about the nutritional value of their products. Usually such claims try to make a connection between the presence of a nutrient, like oat bran, or the absence of a substance, like fat, with a health benefit. Thus the familiar claim that "low-fat" foods are better for the heart.

10   Luckily for consumers, manufacturers who claim their products will make you healthier, or use terms such as "lite," "low-fat," and "high in dietary fiber," had better know

[3] **catchy** – easy to remember

exactly what they're talking about. The Food and Drug Administration (FDA)—the watchdog of the food industry—has set strict guidelines.

11 For many years, there was little control over what food producers could put on product labels or into advertisements. That led to a "free-for-all[4]" of health claims, as one analyst put it. The great oat-bran hype[5] is a good example. A few years ago, some studies indicated that there was a connection between high-fiber diets and a reduced risk of cancer. So, lots of people started eating oat bran because it has a lot of fiber. Many cereal makers wanted to take advantage of the situation. They added a minuscule amount of oat bran to their cereal and truthfully put "Contains Oat Bran!" on the box. Most consumers believed there was a lot of oat bran in the cereal, and sales increased dramatically. The manufacturers had "honestly" tricked the public, and they laughed all the way to the bank.

12 Under present FDA guidelines, that kind of labeling is forbidden. Only health claims supported by strong scientific evidence are permitted. And only products with "significant amounts" are allowed to boast of it on the box.

13 The FDA is also cracking down on other common marketing catchwords[6], like "low sodium" and "low calorie." Under the guidelines, foods must have fewer than 140 milligrams of sodium or fewer than 40 calories per serving to make these claims. A "low-calorie" cookie must contain one-third fewer calories than its regular version.

14 The FTC and FDA guidelines have helped restore some consumer confidence about trusting labels and ads. But, of course, if there's an angle or a loophole, some advertiser will find it. For the smart shopper, the old saying still holds true: Let the buyer beware.

---

[4] **free-for-all** – a situation without limits or controls in which people can do or say what they want

[5] **hype** – attempts to make people think something is good or important by talking about it a lot on television, radio, and so on

[6] **catchword** – a word that is easy to remember and is used frequently

After You Read

Comprehension Check

Read these statements. If a statement is true according to the article, write *T* on the line. If it is false, write *F*. Then write the number of the paragraph that contains the information that helped you make your decision.

_____ 1. The products Americans buy are an expression of their feelings and concerns. (_____)

_____ 2. Some manufacturers believe that what consumers don't know won't hurt them. (_____)

_____ 3. In the past, there was a lot of control over what information could be put on labels and into advertisements. (_____)

_____ 4. Products with a Green Seal logo on them are environmentally friendly. (_____)

_____ 5. American consumers are very concerned about buying healthier and environmentally safer products. (_____)

_____ 6. The FTC has issued stricter guidelines on environmental claims made by manufacturers. (_____)

_____ 7. Health seals are placed on foods that are good for you. (_____)

_____ 8. The FDA has issued stricter guidelines governing what food producers can put on their labels. (_____)

_____ 9. All companies have made real improvements in their products. (_____)

_____ 10. Health claims used in advertising need to be supported by strong scientific evidence. (_____)

Vocabulary Practice

A Choose the word that is closest in meaning to the underlined word in each sentence.

1. The company took a <u>poll</u> to see what percent of its customers preferred low-fat ice cream.
   a. photograph
   b. survey
   c. trip

2. The car manufacturer <u>boasts</u> that its new cars are fuel-efficient.
   a. regrets
   b. denies
   c. claims

3. The government has issued new <u>guidelines</u> for housing permits.
   a. problems
   b. questions
   c. rules

4. Don't <u>exaggerate</u>! I know that car didn't cost $50,000.
   a. overstate
   b. disappoint
   c. oppose

5. It is <u>forbidden</u> to enter this country without a proper visa.
   a. permitted
   b. not permitted
   c. encouraged

6. The <u>strict</u> rules apply to all students at this school.
   a. new
   b. must be obeyed
   c. old-fashioned

7. She made a <u>genuine</u> effort to improve her grades.
   a. real
   b. fake
   c. alarming

8. There is only a <u>minuscule</u> amount of fat in this cereal.
   a. delicious
   b. very large
   c. extremely small

✓ **Learning Idioms**

B These sentences from the article contain idiomatic expressions. Choose the sentence that is closest in meaning to each sentence.

1. Manufacturers got the message loud and clear, and soon big advertisers <u>jumped on the eco-health bandwagon</u>.
   a. When advertisers saw that Americans were concerned about environmental and health issues, they started showing an interest in them, too.
   b. The big advertisers were the first group to become concerned about ecological and health issues.

2. Most manufacturers don't <u>go to these lengths</u>, though that doesn't stop them from making exaggerated claims about the environmental benefits of their products.
   a. Most manufacturers aren't concerned with making products that appeal to environmentally conscious consumers.
   b. Most manufacturers don't do very much to make their products environmentally sensitive, but they still make exaggerated claims about them.

3. Many cereal makers . . . added a minuscule amount of oat bran to their cereal and truthfully put "Contains Oat Bran!" on the box. . . . They <u>laughed all the way to the bank</u>.
   a. By exaggerating the claim about containing oat bran, many cereal makers were able to make a lot of money.
   b. Many cereal makers tried to fool the public with their claims about oat bran but were not able to make much money.

4. The FDA is also <u>cracking down</u> on other common marketing catchwords, like "low sodium" and "low calorie."
   a. The FDA is trying to get rid of words such as "low sodium" and "low calorie."
   b. The FDA is becoming stricter about what kinds of words advertisers use.

A Look at the ad for cereal. How does the company convince people that Honey Hearts is a healthy breakfast food? List the four claims that Yummy Cereals makes about Honey Hearts.

1. _____

2. _____

3. _____

4. _____

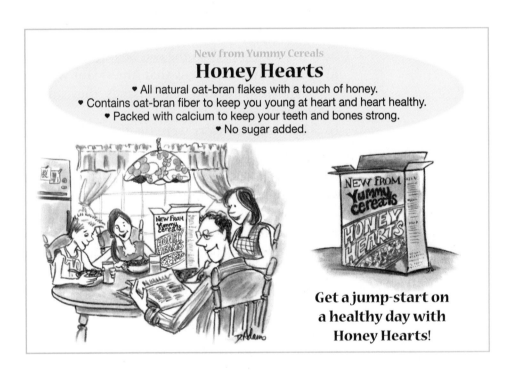

New from Yummy Cereals

Honey Hearts
- All natural oat-bran flakes with a touch of honey.
- Contains oat-bran fiber to keep you young at heart and heart healthy.
- Packed with calcium to keep your teeth and bones strong.
- No sugar added.

Get a jump-start on a healthy day with Honey Hearts!

B Look through several magazines and cut out ads that appeal to environmentally conscious consumers. Make a list of the words, expressions, and slogans the advertisers used to convince the public that their product is environmentally safe. Share your ads and list of slogans with your classmates.

C Now cut out ads that target people who are concerned about their health. What catchwords and slogans do the advertisers use? Share your ads and list of slogans with your classmates.

Choose a Title

Read the article and choose the best title for it. Write the title on the line. Then discuss the questions that follow the article.

1. Roman Gladiators Compete
2. Traditional Advertising Outlets
3. Advertising Goes Digital

_____

by Luria Rittenberg

Methods of advertising have gone through many changes since ancient Romans first put up signs in public areas announcing competitions among gladiators[1]. Even the days of catchy jingles[2] on television seem inadequate when compared to the technological advances of today. Methods of advertising are headed in a completely different direction in the twenty-first century. As the number of buyers looking for information on the Internet increases, so does the number of businesses advertising their products digitally.

Although traditional advertising outlets such as radio, TV, newspapers, and magazines are still popular, Internet advertising is growing rapidly. The benefits are significant, and the creative opportunities for Internet advertising are limitless. In the past, consumers were mainly exposed to ads from large companies with big advertising budgets, while ads from smaller businesses were restricted to local areas. Online, however, even small companies can get an inexpensive website that would show up on a search engine along with the big-name brands. Digitally, they have a better opportunity to expand their product to virtually anyone. No matter how other types of media modernize their advertisements, the Internet has the most important tool to connect with an audience: an interactive experience. Who knows? Maybe if the Roman gladiators had had the access to digital advertising that we have, they would still be battling for audiences today.

[1] **gladiator** – a strong man who fought other men or animals as a public event in ancient Rome
[2] **jingle** – a short song used in television and radio announcements

Today, almost half of North American companies are selling their products online.

1. Do you usually pay attention to online ads? Do you find them useful or annoying?
2. Do you think online ads are an effective way to advertise a product? Why or why not?
3. What kinds of online ads get your attention?

Do's and Taboos

Before You Read

A Discuss these questions with a partner.

1. A *taboo* is something that is forbidden according to custom. Discuss the concept of taboos in your culture. What examples of taboos can you think of?

2. Do you think there is a strong connection between culture and business? What are some ways that culture affects how business is conducted in your country?

3. What kinds of cross-cultural problems might a company encounter when it does business in another country?

✓ **Using Background Knowledge**

B Think about what you know about international business. Read the statements in the chart on the next page. Do you agree or disagree with these statements? Check (✔) your response in the *Before You Read* columns. You will check the last two columns after you read the article.

Before You Read		Statements	After You Read	
AGREE	DISAGREE		AGREE	DISAGREE
		1. What to call people (use of titles, first names, last names) can be confusing in international business relations.		
		2. Attitudes about punctuality vary greatly from one culture to another.		
		3. Colors have different meanings in different cultures.		
		4. Something as simple as a greeting or a smile can be misunderstood.		
		5. Customs about gift-giving are the same all over the world.		
		6. Understanding a country's culture can help a company do business there.		

✓ **Previewing and Predicting**

C Read the four callouts within the article. Use them to make predictions about the kinds of things the author might discuss in the article.

_____

_____

_____

_____

_____

D Learn the meanings of the following words and phrase before you read the article.

heeding (6)	protocol (10)	appropriate (17)
endeavor (6)	abrupt (11)	subtle (22)
crucial (7)	small talk (11)	blunders (24)
punctuality (9)	offensive (16)	

Do's & Taboos

Cultural Aspects of International Business

by M. Katherine Glover

The traditional Thai greeting, the wai

Adapting to cultural variables is a significant part of any international business endeavor.

1 Never touch the head of a Thai or pass an object over it, as the head is considered sacred in Thailand. Likewise, never point the bottoms of the feet in the direction of another person in Thailand or cross your legs while sitting, especially in the presence of an older person.

2 Avoid using triangular shapes in Hong Kong, Korea, or Taiwan, as the triangle is considered a negative shape in those countries.

3 Remember that the number 7 is considered bad luck in Kenya and good luck in the Czech Republic and has magical connotations in Benin.

4 Red is a positive color in Denmark but represents witchcraft and death in many African countries.

5 A nod means "no" in Bulgaria, and shaking the head side-to-side means "yes."

6 Understanding and heeding cultural variables such as these is one of the most significant aspects of being successful in any international business endeavor. A lack of familiarity with the business practices, social customs, and etiquette of a country can weaken a company's position in the market, prevent it from accomplishing its objectives, and ultimately lead to failure.

7 As business has become increasingly international and communications technology continues to develop, the need for clearly understood communication between members of different cultures is even more crucial. Growing competition for international markets is another reason that companies must consider cultural distinctions. Business executives who are not alert to cultural differences simply cannot function efficiently overseas. They may not even understand something as basic as what signifies closing a deal in a particular country—a handshake, a written contract, or a Memorandum of Understanding[1].

8 Taking the time to learn something about the culture of a country before doing business there is a show of respect and is usually deeply appreciated, not to mention rewarding for the company. Those who understand the culture are more likely to develop successful, long-term business relationships.

---

[1] **Memorandum of Understanding** – a legal document outlining the terms and details of an agreement between parties, including each party's requirements and responsibilities

9 Customs vary widely from one country to another. Something with one meaning in one area may mean the opposite somewhere else. Some of the cultural variables that firms most often face include differences in the development of business relationships, attitudes toward punctuality, greeting styles, significance of gestures, customs regarding names and titles, gift-giving customs, business cards, negotiating, and meanings of colors and numbers.

10 Firms must pay close attention to differences in the degree of importance placed on developing business relationships. In some countries, businesspeople have a very direct style, while in others they are much more personal in style. Many nationalities value the personal relationship more than most Americans do in business. In these countries, long-term relationships based on trust are necessary for doing business. Many U.S. firms make the mistake of rushing into business discussions and "coming on too strong" instead of nurturing the relationship first. According to Roger Axtell in his book *Do's and Taboos of Hosting International Visitors*, "There is much more to business than just business in many parts of the world. Socializing, friendships, etiquette, grace, patience, and protocol are integral parts of business." He feels that jumping right into business discussions before getting acquainted can be a "bad mistake."

11 Charles Ford, commercial attaché in Guatemala, cites this cultural distinction as the greatest area of difference between the American and Guatemalan styles of doing business. The inexperienced American visitor, he claims, often tries to force a business relationship. The abrupt "always watching the clock" style rarely works in Guatemala. A better-informed business executive would, he advises, engage in small talk about Guatemala, indicate an interest in the families of his or her business associates, join them for lunch or dinner, and generally allow time for a personal relationship to develop. Solid business opportunities usually follow a strong personal relationship in Guatemala. This holds true for Latin America in general.

Learning about a country's culture is a show of respect and is usually appreciated.

---

12 Building a personal rapport is also important when doing business in Greece, according to Sondra Snowdon, president of Snowdon's International Protocol, Inc., a firm that trains and prepares executives in cross-cultural communications. Business entertaining is usually done in the evening at a local *taverna*, and spouses are often included. The relaxed atmosphere is important to building a business relationship based on friendship. Belgians, however, are the opposite, Snowdon says. They are likely to get down to business right away and are unusually conservative and efficient in their approach to business meetings.

13 Attitudes toward punctuality vary greatly from one culture to another and unless understood can cause confusion and misunderstanding. Romanians, Japanese, and Germans are very punctual, while many people in Latin countries have a more relaxed attitude toward time. The Japanese consider it rude to be late for a business meeting, but it is acceptable, even fashionable, to be late for a social occasion. In Guatemala, on the other hand, according to Ford, a luncheon at a specified time means that some guests might be 10 minutes early, while others might be 45 minutes late.

14 When crossing cultural lines, something as simple as a greeting can be misunderstood. The form of greeting differs from culture to culture. Traditional greetings may be a handshake, hug, nose rub, kiss, placement of the hands in a praying position, or various

other gestures. Lack of awareness concerning the country's accepted form of greeting can lead to awkward encounters. The Japanese bow is one of the most well-known forms of greeting. The bow symbolizes respect and humility and is a very important custom to observe when doing business with the Japanese. There are also different levels of bowing, each with a significant meaning. Japanese and Americans often combine a handshake with a bow so that each culture may show the other respect. Handshakes are the accepted form of greeting in Italy. Italians use a handshake for greetings and good-byes. Unlike in the United States, men do not stand when a woman enters or leaves a room, and they do not kiss a woman's hand. The latter is reserved for royalty. The traditional Thai greeting, the *wai*, is made by placing both hands together in a prayer position at the chin and bowing slightly. The higher the hands, the more respect is symbolized. Failure to return a *wai* greeting is equivalent to refusing to shake hands in the West.

When crossing cultural lines, something as simple as a greeting can be misunderstood.

---

15 According to Snowdon, American intentions are often misunderstood and Americans are sometimes perceived as not meaning what they say. For example, in Denmark the standard American greeting, "Hi, how are you?" leads the Danes to think the U.S. businessperson really wants to know how they are. She suggests that "Hi, I'm pleased to meet you" is preferable and conveys a more sincere message.

16 People around the world use body movements or gestures to convey specific messages. Though countries sometimes use the same gestures, they often have very different meanings. Misunderstandings over gestures is a common occurrence in cross-cultural communication, and misinterpretation along these lines can lead to business complications and social embarrassment. The "OK" sign commonly used in the United States is a good example of a gesture that has several different meanings according to the country. In France, it means "zero"; in Japan, it is a symbol for money; and in Brazil, it is an offensive gesture that has a vulgar[2] connotation.

17 Proper use of names and titles is often a source of confusion in international business relations. In many countries (including the United Kingdom, France, and Denmark), it is appropriate to use titles until use of first names is suggested. First names are seldom used when doing business in Germany. Visiting businesspeople should use the surname preceded by the title. Titles such as "Herr Direktor" are sometimes used to indicate prestige, status, and rank. Thais, on the other hand, address each other by first names and reserve last names for very formal occasions or written communications. When using the first name, they often use the honorific "Khun" or a title preceding it.

18 Customs concerning gift-giving are extremely important to understand. In some cultures, gifts are expected, and failure to present them is considered an insult, whereas in other countries offering a gift is considered offensive. Business executives also need to know when to present gifts—on the initial visit or afterwards; where to present gifts—in public or private; what type of gift to present; what color it should be; and how many to present.

19 Gift-giving is an important part of doing business in Japan. Exchanging gifts symbolizes the depth and strength of a

---

2 vulgar – very rude and offensive, often relating to sex

business relationship to the Japanese. Gifts are usually exchanged at the first meeting. When presented with a gift, companies are expected to respond by giving a gift. In sharp contrast, gifts are rarely exchanged in Germany and are usually not appropriate. Small gifts are fine, but expensive items are not a general practice. Gift-giving is not a normal custom in Belgium or the United Kingdom either, although in both countries, flowers are a suitable gift if invited to someone's home. Even that is not as easy as it sounds. International executives must use caution to choose appropriate flowers. For example, avoid sending chrysanthemums (especially white ones) in Belgium and elsewhere in Europe, since they are mainly used for funerals. In Europe, it is also considered bad luck to present an even number of flowers. Beware of white flowers in Japan, where they are associated with death, as purple flowers are in Mexico and Brazil.

20   Yue-Sai Kan, host and executive producer of a television show about Asia, *Looking East*, and of a new four-part series, *Doing Business in Asia*, points out that customs regarding the exchange of business cards vary, too. Seemingly minor in importance, observance of a country's customs regarding card-giving is a key part of business protocol.

21   In Japan, it is particularly important to be aware of the way business cards should be exchanged, according to Yue-Sai Kan. The Western tradition of accepting a business card and immediately putting it in your pocket is considered very rude there, she contends. Rather, the proper approach is to carefully look at the card after accepting it, observe the title and organization, acknowledge with a nod that you have digested the information, and perhaps make a relevant comment or ask a polite question. During a meeting, spread the cards in front of you relating to where people are sitting. In other words, says Yue-Sai Kan, treat a business card as you would

treat its owner—with respect. When presenting a card in either Japan or South Korea, it is important to use both hands and position the card so that the recipient can read it. In any country where English is not commonly taught, the information should be printed in the native language on the reverse side of the card.

22   Negotiating can be a complex process between parties from the same nation. Negotiating across cultures is even more complicated because of the added chance of misunderstandings stemming from cultural differences. When negotiating, a host of cultural variables must be dealt with all at once. For example, it is essential to understand the importance of rank in the other country and to know who the decision makers are. It is equally important to be familiar with the business style of the foreign company. Is it important to be direct or subtle? Is it necessary to have an established relationship with the company before beginning negotiations? Executives negotiating with foreign companies must also understand the nature of agreements in the country, the significance of gestures, and the etiquette of negotiations.

23   These cultural variables are examples of the things that men and women involved in international business must be aware of. At times in the past, Americans have not had a good track record of being sensitive to cultural distinctions. However, as business has become more global, Americans have become more sensitive to cultural differences and the importance of dealing with them effectively. Still, some companies fail to do their homework and make fatal or near-fatal mistakes that could have easily been prevented. A number of firms have learned the hard way that successful domestic strategies do not necessarily work overseas and that business must be adapted to the culture.

> *Failure to research and understand a culture has led to many international business blunders.*

24   Failure to research and understand a culture before entering the market has led to many international business blunders. They run the gamut from forgivable to disastrous. Some years ago, for example, a leading U.S. golf ball manufacturer targeted Japan as an important new market for golf. Yet sales of the company's golf balls were well below average. The firm, as it turned out, had packaged the balls in groups of four—the number of death in Japan.

25   Mistakes of these types can at the least reduce sales, and at the worst, give the company and the product such a bad name that it closes out the market entirely. To avoid blunders like this, a company ultimately must not only have a sensitivity to other cultures but also must have a good understanding of its own culture and how other countries see American culture. ■

After You Read

Comprehension Check

A Answer these questions.

1. What problems can a lack of familiarity with the business practices and social customs of a country cause a company?

_____

_____

_____

2. What are some of the cultural differences that firms must address when doing business in other countries?

_____

_____

_____

3. What would a well-informed businessperson do to promote a successful business relationship in Latin American countries such as Guatemala?

_____

_____

_____

4. What are some traditional forms of greetings?

_____

_____

_____

5. What can companies do to avoid blunders in business?

_____

_____

_____

Taking Notes

B The article describes the cultural variables that firms most often face. Read the article again. This time, take notes on the article by completing the two-column notes below.

Cultural Variable	Details/Examples
1. Development of business relationships	—Difference between American and Guatemalan business styles: Inexperienced Americans—may force a business relationship. Better-informed Americans—allow time for a personal relationship to develop. Solid business opportunities usually follow a strong personal relationship in Guatemala. —In Greece building a personal rapport is important when doing business. Belgians are the opposite and get down to business right away.
2. Attitudes toward punctuality	
3. Greeting styles	
4. Significance of gestures	
5. Customs regarding names and titles	
6. Gift-giving customs	
7. Business cards	
8. Meaning of colors and numbers	

Understanding Contrast

Authors often **contrast** people, events, things, or ideas in order to explain how they are different. English uses many special words and phrases to show contrast. Look for these signal words and phrases that show contrasts.

but	nevertheless	rather
conversely	nonetheless	yet
however	on the contrary	
in contrast	on the other hand	

C Answer these questions about the differences in business practices in different countries. Use a signal word or phrase in each answer.

1. What is the difference between gift-giving etiquette in Japan and Germany?

   _____

   _____

2. What is the difference between the proper use of names and titles in Thailand and the United Kingdom?

   _____

   _____

3. How does the meaning of the "OK" sign differ in the United States and France?

   _____

   _____

4. How are the attitudes toward punctuality different between people from Japan and people from Latin countries?

   _____

   _____

5. What is the difference between the meaning of the number 7 in Kenya and the Czech Republic?

   _____

   _____

D Look at the statements in the chart on page 223 again and mark *Agree* or *Disagree* for each one in the *After You Read* columns. Talk to a partner about why any of your new responses differed from the ones made before you read the article.

A **Circle the correct answer.**

1. Which is an example of a business <u>endeavor</u>?
   a. opening a store in another country
   b. planning a vacation

2. Which is an example of business <u>protocol</u> in Japan?
   a. being late for a meeting
   b. following the rules of giving and receiving business cards

3. If you are usually <u>punctual</u> for meetings, you are _____.
   a. late
   b. on time

4. If certain behaviors are considered <u>offensive</u>, you should _____.
   a. do them as much as possible
   b. avoid doing them

5. If it is <u>appropriate</u> to call your mother's friend by her first name, you
   _____.
   a. can call her by her first name
   b. shouldn't call her by her first name

6. If you make a serious <u>blunder</u>, you should _____.
   a. apologize
   b. say thank you

7. If you engage in <u>small talk</u> with your friends, you are probably talking
   about _____.
   a. things that are not very important
   b. very serious matters

8. People who <u>heed</u> the rules of social etiquette _____.
   a. don't care about the accepted rules of social behavior
   b. care about the accepted rules of social behavior

9. If there is a <u>subtle</u> difference between two plans, the plans are_____.
   a. obviously different
   b. slightly different

10. If it is <u>crucial</u> to get someone to the hospital immediately, you should
    _____.
    a. take your time getting her there
    b. get her there in a hurry

11. If someone has an <u>abrupt</u> manner, he is probably not very _____.
    a. friendly
    b. intelligent

B For each pair of words, circle *S* if they are synonyms or *A* if they are antonyms.

1. small talk	conversation	*S*	*A*
2. subtle	obvious	*S*	*A*
3. crucial	unimportant	*S*	*A*
4. abrupt	friendly	*S*	*A*
5. punctuality	lateness	*S*	*A*
6. protocol	procedure	*S*	*A*
7. blunder	mistake	*S*	*A*
8. offensive	rude	*S*	*A*
9. endeavor	venture	*S*	*A*
10. appropriate	unacceptable	*S*	*A*
11. heed	disregard	*S*	*A*

✓ **Recognizing Commonly Confused Words**

Study the words in the list.

Word	Meaning/Use	Example
accept	to take something that someone else offers you	*I hope he **accepts** the job offer.*
except	but	*I like all kinds of movies **except** horror films.*
affect	(verb) to influence	*Lack of sleep **affects** your mood.*
effect	(noun) result	*The snowstorm had a big **effect** on the city.*
cite	to quote or name the source of something	*I **cited** several quotes from the same author in my report.*
sight	vision	*The doctors were able to save her **sight**.*
site	a position or place	*The new office building was built on the **site** of the old library.*
precede	to go before	*Jason **preceded** me as president of the club.*
proceed	to go forward	*It's time to **proceed** with the ceremony.*

principal	(adjective) most important	*His **principal** reason for moving was to be near his work.*
principle	(noun) a general or basic truth	*The **principle** of gravity is important in physics.*
weak	not strong	*She felt very **weak** after her long illness.*
week	the seven-day period from Sunday to Saturday	*There are 52 **weeks** in a year.*
weather	condition of the air or atmosphere	*The **weather** here is nice in the summer.*
whether	(conjunction, shows choice) if	*Tell me **whether** or not you want to go home.*
whose	(possessive form of *who*)	*I don't know **whose** car this is.*
who's	(contraction of *who is*)	***Who's** riding in my car with me?*

C Complete each sentence with a word from the list. Be sure to use the correct form of the words.

1. A yellow light means _____ with caution.

2. You need to _____ all the articles you used to write this report.

3. This medicine _____ your heart.

4. You can borrow any of my sweaters _____ my new yellow one.

5. I believe in the _____ that all people deserve equal treatment under the law.

6. I don't care _____ we stay home or go to the movies.

7. Sarah felt _____ for several _____ after her illness.

8. Do you know _____ book this is?

Discuss these questions as a class.

1. Do businesspeople in your culture have a more direct style or a more personal style?
2. Misunderstandings often result from trying to communicate in a foreign language. Have you ever tried to express something in another language that resulted in a misunderstanding? Was it funny? Embarrassing? Frustrating? If so, share your story with the class.

Read the article and choose the best title for it. Write the title on the line. Then discuss the questions that follow the article.

1. Colors Communicate
2. Lucky Colors
3. Green Guarantees Sales
4. An Expensive Lesson

Hong Kong is a city inclined toward red; in Thailand the color is yellow; India leans toward reds and oranges. These are not political colors, but colors that connote religious beliefs.

To an Asian, colors are associated with beliefs, religious and otherwise. To the Chinese, red is very lucky, but to Thais, yellow brings good fortune. The combination of blue, black, and white is, to the Chinese, suggestive of a funeral.

Many Western businesspeople believe that most Asians have become Westernized in their outlook. This is true in part. But Westernization and education do not usually completely replace the culture and beliefs passed down by an Asian's forefathers. They tend instead to make an intricate alliance between his cultural and religious bonds. The approach required to sell an Asian any commodity must follow the basic formula of considering national pride, acknowledging equality, and understanding the Asian's beliefs.

Advertisers are advised to take into consideration the religious and superstitious beliefs connected with colors before using them. But color can be a touchy thing. The color combinations of green and purple are acceptable throughout Asia, as these colors were worn by religious leaders in earlier times. However, using one or both of these colors is no guarantee of sales, as a prominent manufacturer of water-recreation products learned in Malaysia. Its home office received heated requests from its Malaysian distributors to stop shipments on all products colored green. The distributors reported that numerous customers associated the color green with the jungle and illness!

1. What are the meanings of specific colors such as red, white, blue, green, and black in your culture?
2. How do colors have an impact on doing business in your culture?

Tie It All Together

Discussion

Discuss these questions in a small group.

1. What advice would you give someone who plans to do business in your country?
2. Think about some of your recent purchases. What kinds of things influenced your purchasing decisions? What are some factors you take into account when you buy something?
3. Are you loyal to certain brands? If so, which ones?
4. Do you have business experience that lets you think about these and other questions from a businessperson's point of view as well as a consumer's point of view? If so, what kind of business experience do you have?

Just For Fun

Answer these questions.

1. There are two doors. Behind one of the doors is a dead end. Behind the other door is the path you are looking for. There is a guard in front of each door. One of the guards always tells the truth, but the other guard always lies. What question can you ask either guard so you can find out which door you should go through?

2. Look at the way the letters of the Roman alphabet are written below. Some of the letters are above the line and some are below it. Figure out the guideline and put the letter *Z* in the correct position.

A   EF   HI   KLMN   T   VWXY
—————————————————————————————————————
BCD   G   J   OPQRS   U

3. Three sets of twins each have a garden. The twins' names are Daisy, Heather, Ivy, Lily, Rose, and Violet. Each garden has two kinds of flowers in it. In her garden, each twin has a flower with the same name as one of the other twins, not her own twin. Rose's garden has daisies, but Daisy's garden doesn't have roses. Heather grows ivy, and Ivy grows flowers that have the same name as Violet's twin sister, who is not Daisy. No two women whose names end in the letter *y* are sisters. Name the three sets of twins and the flowers they grow.

Kids and Food

Childhood obesity is on the rise, and that means many children are overweight and at risk for health problems. This video reports on companies that use popular characters from television shows to market unhealthy food to children. Currently it is up to the companies to make changes and put health before profit, but many believe the federal government should create strict guidelines to prevent companies from marketing unhealthy products to kids. When you shop for groceries, have you ever noticed packages that would attract kids' attention? What kinds of products are marketed to children?

A Study these words. Then watch the video.

altruistic	epidemic	status quo
assume a role	external pressures	tackle
ban	obesity	viable
bombarded	regulations	voluntary measures

B Read these questions and then watch the video again. Write an answer to each question.

1. According to the video, what role could food and media companies have in the childhood-obesity epidemic?

_____

_____

2. According to Marva Smalls of Nickelodeon, why would food and media companies want to make changes and market healthier foods to kids?

_____

_____

3. Does Margo Wootan of the consumer-rights group agree? Does she think companies will reform advertising practices on their own?

_____

_____

4. According to the video, what is the attitude of food and media companies when it comes to consumer choices?

_____

_____

C Discuss these questions with a partner or in a small group.

1. What do you think about the issue of marketing unhealthy foods to children? Should consumers be better protected, perhaps by restrictions from the government, or should companies be free to label products to maximize sales?
2. Have you ever heard the phrase "buyer beware"? Explain in your own words what the expression means.

Reader's Journal

Think about the topics and ideas you have read about and discussed in this unit. Pick a topic from the following list, choose one of the discussion questions in the unit, or write about an idea of your own. Write about it for ten to twenty minutes.

- how your purchasing decisions are influenced by the ads you see, hear, or read
- business styles in your culture
- the meaning of colors in your culture
- gift-giving customs in your culture

Vocabulary Self-Test

Complete each sentence with the correct word or phrase.

A
blunders	poll	small talk
boasts	protocol	strict
heed	punctuality	subtle

1. The company _____ that all of its products are friendly to the environment.

2. I don't enjoy dinner parties where I have to make _____ with people I don't really know.

3. The school has _____ rules about cheating.

4. We took a _____ to see how many people exercise every day.

5. She got sick because she didn't _____ her doctor's warnings.

6. I think it's rude to be late. In our family, _____ is very important.

7. Misunderstanding cultural variables such as the meaning of colors and numbers has caused many advertising _____.

8. Standing when the judge enters is a part of courtroom _____.

9. The poem has a _____ meaning. You have to read it several times to understand it.

B
abrupt	exaggerates	minuscule
appropriate	forbidden	offensive
crucial	genuine	
endeavor	guidelines	

1. His _____ manner of dealing with people makes me uncomfortable. He should try to be more friendly.

2. A gesture that may be perfectly acceptable in one culture may be quite _____ in another.

3. We made a(n) _____ effort to be nice to our new neighbors so they would feel at home here.

4. I don't think this movie is _____ for children because there is so much violence.

5. He put such a(n) _____ amount of sugar in my coffee that I can hardly taste it.

6. Smoking on airplanes is strictly _____. It is dangerous and illegal.

7. Our teacher has certain _____ for how to write a report.

8. It is _____ to understand cultural variables before you undertake an international business _____.

9. My sister always _____ the truth when she tells a story, and I never know how much to believe.

Vocabulary Self-Tests Answer Key

Unit 1
(pages 33–34)

A 1. revitalize
2. artificial
3. evolved
4. vision
5. submit/sloppy
6. neglect
7. humiliated

B 1. alarming
2. abandon
3. multiple
4. exception
5. qualms/worthwhile
6. embrace
7. ups and downs

C 1. risky
2. rough
3. bewildered
4. daring
5. feat
6. advocate
7. participants

Unit 2
(pages 63–64)

A 1. remarkably
2. awesome
3. skeptical
4. prevailing/fluctuate
5. misguided
6. persists
7. illustrious
8. adversity

B 1. brilliant
2. savvy
3. stick to
4. pastel/wardrobe

5. irritable
6. turmoil
7. perpetual

C 1. trite
2. modest
3. upbeat
4. abundance
5. agonized
6. cynical
7. no-brainer
8. contagious
9. illusion

Unit 3
(pages 91–92)

A 1. stunned
2. novels
3. for the time being
4. sturdy
5. insignificant
6. refuge
7. swollen

B 1. landlord/Laundromat
2. strong-willed
3. crumble
4. peers
5. dream up
6. dissuade
7. intense

C 1. easygoing
2. conventional
3. conscientious
4. rebellious
5. sociable
6. strive
7. diplomatic
8. absurd

Unit 4
(pages 122–123)

A 1. down the road
2. stick with it
3. high-profile
4. mentor
5. equivalent
6. potential
7. keep her cool
8. take it in stride

B 1. get caught up in
2. spectators/cheered
3. perseverance
4. flaw
5. distracted
6. tactics

C 1. collapse/exhaustion
2. delight
3. consultation
4. triumph
5. suspense
6. trigger
7. running neck and neck

Unit 5
(pages 155–156)

A 1. medicinal/remedy
2. hooked up to
3. enhance
4. affectionately
5. recovering
6. disorders
7. supplemental

B 1. beneficial
2. straight
3. moderate
4. stimulate

5. adaptation
6. promotes/combat
7. well-being

C 1. wound
2. unpalatable
3. toxins/predators
4. defenses
5. therapeutic
6. potent
7. distinguished

Unit 6
(pages 183–184)

A 1. confessed
2. legitimate
3. penalty
4. obscure
5. convicted/witnesses
6. evidence
7. guilty
8. get away with

B 1. make or break
2. dreadful
3. pulled off
4. Poachers
5. monotonous
6. ransom
7. disaster
8. smuggled

C 1. concealed
2. crack down on
3. astute
4. wear and tear
5. on the brink of
6. tracking down
7. traffic

Unit 7
(pages 211–212)

A 1. monitor
2. boost
3. device
4. precise
5. apparent
6. optimum
7. distinction
8. anticipate
9. arbitrary

B 1. indefinable
2. misconception
3. are into
4. durable
5. resistant
6. ironed out
7. collaborators
8. specialized

C 1. shelter
2. composition

3. gravity
4. mission
5. automated
6. rotation
7. spin-offs

Unit 8
(pages 238–239)

A 1. boasts
2. small talk
3. strict
4. poll
5. heed
6. punctuality
7. blunders
8. protocol
9. subtle

B 1. abrupt
2. offensive
3. genuine
4. appropriate
5. miniscule
6. forbidden
7. guidelines
8. crucial/endeavor
9. exaggerates

Glossary

A

abandon (20): to give up something that was your responsibility

abrupt (223): brief and making no effort to be friendly

absurd (72): ridiculous

abundance (36): a large quantity

adaptation (142): a physical characteristic that has evolved to allow plants and animals to survive in their environment

adversity (44): difficulties or problems that seem to be caused by bad luck

advocate (11): someone who supports something

affectionately (126): in a way that shows feelings of warmth or love

agonize (36): to worry about

alarming (20): causing fear

anticipate (186): to imagine or expect that something will happen

apparent (201): able to be easily seen or understood

appropriate (223): acceptable or right for a particular situation or occasion

arbitrary (201): based on chance rather than being planned or based on reason

artificial (11): made by human beings, not natural

astute (166): clever and intelligent, having good judgment

automated (194): operated by machines or computers

awesome (36): so impressive that it makes you feel awe; extremely good (*slang*)

B

be into something (201): to be interested in or involved with something

beneficial (142): producing a good effect

bewildered (3): confused

blunder (223): a big mistake, often caused by lack of care or thought

boast (215): to claim something is true

boost (194): an improvement or increase in something

brilliant (44): exceptionally intelligent or skilled

C

cheer (94): to give a loud shout of approval or encouragement

collaborator (194): someone working with others to achieve something

collapse (102): to fall down from weakness

combat (142): to try to stop something unpleasant or harmful from happening

composition (194): the parts, substances, etc., that something is made of

concealed (173): hidden

confess (158): to admit to committing a crime

conscientious (79): showing a lot of care and attention; putting a lot of effort into your work

consultation (112): a meeting to discuss something or to get advice

contagious (36): transmitted from one person to another

conventional (79): traditional and ordinary

convict (158): to prove that someone has committed a crime

crack down on (173): to take strong action against illegal activities

crucial (223): very important or significant

crumbling (66): breaking into small pieces

cynical (36): believing that people are interested only in themselves and are not sincere

D

daring (3): courageous and taking risks

defense (142): things that provide protection against attack

delight (102): pleasure, joy, or happiness

device (186): an object that has been invented to fulfill a particular purpose

diplomatic (79): good at dealing with people in a way that causes no bad feelings

disaster (166): an event that causes harm, damage, or death

disorder (133): an illness of the mind or body

dissuade (72): to convince someone not to do something

distinction (201): a difference between two similar things

distinguished (133): well-known and respected

distracted (94): showing lack of concentration

down the road (112): in the future

dreadful (173): awful

dream up (66): to invent or imagine something

durable (186): able to last a long time without becoming damaged

E

easygoing (79): relaxed, not easily upset

embrace (11): to eagerly accept ideas and opinions

endeavor (223): an earnest attempt

enhance (133): to improve the quality, amount, or strength of something

equivalent (112): having the same amount, value, or qualities

evidence (158): objects or information used to prove that someone is guilty or innocent

evolved (3): developed by gradually changing

exaggerate (215): to make something seem larger, more important, better, or worse than it really is

exception (11): something that does not fit into the general rules

exhaustion (102): a feeling of extreme tiredness

F

feat (3): an accomplishment

flaw (94): a fault, mistake, or weakness

fluctuate (44): to change from high to low levels

for the time being (66): now

forbidden (215): not permitted; prohibited

G

genuine (215): having the qualities that are claimed

get away with (166): to avoid punishment for something

get caught up in (94): to become involved in something unintentionally

gravity (194): the force which attracts objects toward one another

guidelines (215): official recommendations about how something should be done

guilty (158): responsible for a crime

H

heed (223): to pay attention to something, especially advice or a warning

high-profile (94): attracting a lot of attention from people

hooked up to (133): connected to

humiliate (3): to make someone feel ashamed by making him or her seem stupid or weak

I

illusion (44): a false idea or belief

illustrious (44): famous and well-respected

indefinable (201): impossible to clearly describe or explain

insignificant (72): unimportant

intense (79): very serious, and usually having strong emotions or opinions

iron out (194): to remove problems

irritable (52): easily annoyed

K

keep one's cool (94): to stay calm

L

landlord (66): a person who owns a building that people pay to use

Laundromat (66): a place with washing machines where you pay to do your laundry

legitimate (158): complying with the law

M

make or break (166): resulting in great success or complete failure

medicinal (126): refers to substances that are used to cure illnesses

mentor (94): someone who gives other people advice and teaches them how to do their job

minuscule (215): extremely small

misconception (201): a wrong idea

misguided (44): based on mistaken ideas

mission (194): a special trip made by a spacecraft or military aircraft

moderate (133): not large, great, or severe

modest (44): not large or extreme

monitor (186): to watch and check the progress of something

monotonous (166): staying the same and not changing and therefore boring

multiple (20): many

N

neglect (20): to fail to give care or attention to something or someone

no-brainer (44): an idea that is so easily understood or done that it requires no thought (*slang*)

novel (72): a long printed story about imaginary characters and events

O

obscure (158): not well-known

offensive (223): rude, showing lack of respect

on the brink of (173): likely that something will happen soon

optimum (186): the best out of a number of possible alternatives

P

participant (11): someone who takes part in something

pastel (52): a pale, soft color

peers (79): people who are the same age or have the same social position

penalty (158): a legal punishment such as a fine

perpetual (44): continuing all the time without changing

perseverance (94): continued effort and determination

persist (36): to continue despite problems

poacher (173): somebody who hunts animals illegally

poll (215): a study in which people are asked for their opinions about a subject or person

potent (126): powerful or effective

potential (112): the ability to develop, achieve, or succeed

precise (201): exact

predator (142): an animal that hunts and eats other animals in order to survive

prevailing (36): very common in a particular place at a particular time

promote (126): to support something and help it become successful

protocol (223): the rules of behavior in official occasions

pull off (158): to succeed in accomplishing something

punctuality (223): being on time

Q

qualm (3): a doubt

R

ransom (158): money that is demanded in exchange for someone or something obtained illegally

rebellious (79): opposing authority

recovering (133): getting better after an illness

refuge (72): a safe place that gives protection from danger

remarkably (36): surprisingly

remedy (126): a cure

resistant (186): not harmed or affected by something

revitalize (20): to give new life or energy to something

risky (3): dangerous

rotation (201): the turning of something in a circle, especially around a fixed point

rough (3): approximate

running neck and neck (102): very close in a race

savvy (52): having practical knowledge and ability

shelter (194): something (such as a building or tent) that protects you from the weather

skeptical (36): tending not to believe things but to question them

sloppy (20): filled with mistakes; not neat or careful

small talk (223): a conversation about unimportant things

smuggle (173): to carry illegal goods into a country

sociable (79): friendly and liking to be with other people

specialized (186): developed for a particular purpose or job

spectators (102): people watching an event

spin-off (186): a product that develops from another product

stick to (52): to decide what to do, say, or believe and not change it

stick with it (112): to continue to do something

stimulate (126): to help a process develop or work faster

straight (133): following one after another without interruption

strict (215): needing to be closely obeyed

strive (79): to try very hard to do something

strong-willed (72): determined to do what you want

stunned (72): very surprised about something

sturdy (72): physically strong and solid

submit (20): to give to someone in authority, like a teacher

subtle (223): not obvious

supplemental (133): additional

suspense (102): a feeling of excitement when you are waiting for something to happen

swollen (66): larger than usual

tactic (112): a method

take something in stride (94): to deal with a problem calmly without getting annoyed or upset

therapeutic (126): used in the treatment of disease

toxin (142): a poisonous substance

track down (173): to find a person, animal, or object by searching or following a trail

trafficking (173): an illegal trade in goods

trigger (112): to cause something to happen

trite (44): overused and unoriginal

triumph (102): an important success

turmoil (52): a state of confusion

unpalatable (142): unpleasant to taste or eat

upbeat (36): full of optimism or cheerfulness

ups and downs (11): good times and bad times

V

vision (11): a dream

W

wardrobe (52): all the clothes that belong to a person

wear and tear (166): damage caused by using something over a period of time

well-being (126): a feeling of being healthy and happy

witness (166): someone who saw or heard something related to a crime

worthwhile (3): valuable; worth all the time, effort, or money you have used

wound (142): an injury to the skin

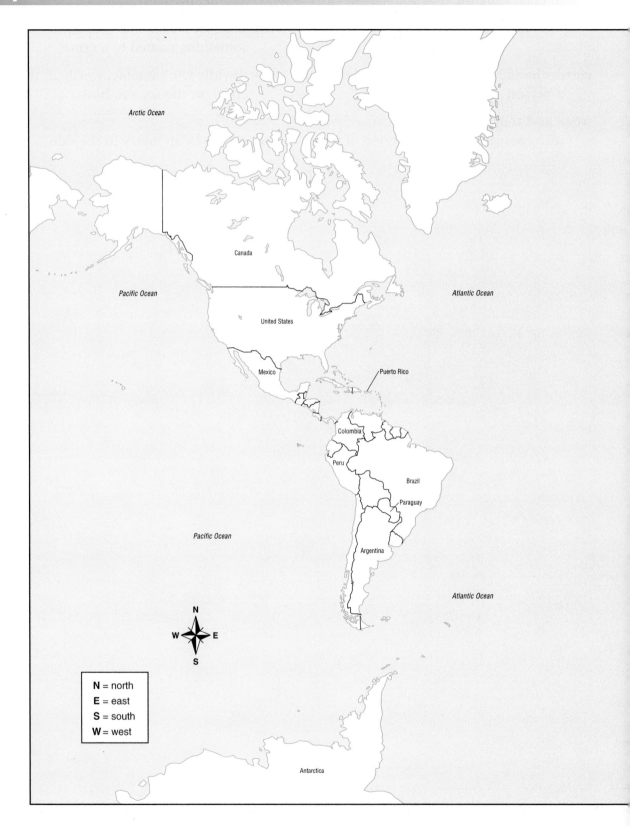

Arctic Ocean

Canada

Pacific Ocean

Atlantic Ocean

United States

Mexico

Puerto Rico

Colombia

Peru

Brazil

Paraguay

Pacific Ocean

Argentina

Atlantic Ocean

N
W + E
S

N = north
E = east
S = south
W = west

Antarctica

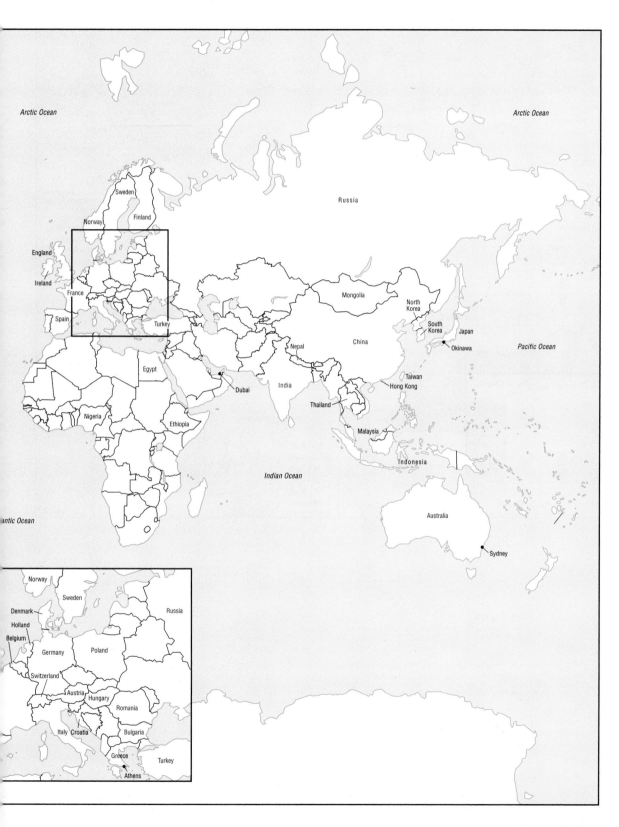

Arctic Ocean

Arctic Ocean

Russia

Sweden

Norway   Finland

England

Ireland

France

Spain

Turkey

Mongolia

North
Korea

South
Korea   Japan

Okinawa

Pacific Ocean

Egypt

Nepal

China

Taiwan

Hong Kong

Dubai

India

Nigeria

Thailand

Ethiopia

Malaysia

Indonesia

Indian Ocean

antic Ocean

Australia

Sydney

Norway

Sweden

Russia

Denmark

Holland

Belgium

Germany   Poland

Switzerland

Austria

Hungary

Romania

Italy Croatia

Bulgaria

Greece

Turkey

Athens

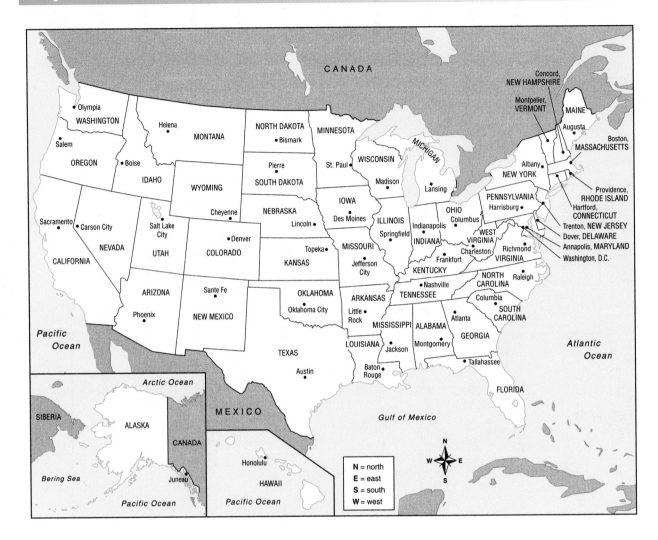

Concord, NEW HAMPSHIRE
Montpelier, VERMONT
MAINE
Augusta
Boston, MASSACHUSETTS
Albany
NEW YORK
Providence, RHODE ISLAND
Hartford, CONNECTICUT
Trenton, NEW JERSEY
Dover, DELAWARE
Annapolis, MARYLAND
Washington, D.C.

CANADA

Olympia
WASHINGTON
Salem
OREGON
Helena
MONTANA
Boise
IDAHO
NORTH DAKOTA
Bismark
MINNESOTA
St. Paul
WISCONSIN
Madison
MICHIGAN
Lansing
PENNSYLVANIA
Harrisburg
Pierre
SOUTH DAKOTA
WYOMING
Cheyenne
NEBRASKA
IOWA
Des Moines
ILLINOIS
Springfield
INDIANA
Indianapolis
OHIO
Columbus
WEST VIRGINIA
Charleston
VIRGINIA
Richmond
Sacramento
Carson City
NEVADA
Salt Lake City
UTAH
Denver
COLORADO
Lincoln
KANSAS
Topeka
MISSOURI
Jefferson City
KENTUCKY
Frankfort
NORTH CAROLINA
Raleigh
CALIFORNIA
ARIZONA
Phoenix
Sante Fe
NEW MEXICO
OKLAHOMA
Oklahoma City
ARKANSAS
Little Rock
TENNESSEE
Nashville
SOUTH CAROLINA
Columbia
Pacific Ocean
Atlantic Ocean
MISSISSIPPI
ALABAMA
Atlanta
GEORGIA
Montgomery
LOUISIANA
Jackson
TEXAS
Austin
Baton Rouge
Tallahassee
FLORIDA
Gulf of Mexico

MEXICO

Arctic Ocean
SIBERIA
ALASKA
CANADA
Bering Sea
Juneau
Pacific Ocean

Honolulu
HAWAII
Pacific Ocean

N = north
E = east
S = south
W = west

N
W E
S

Unit 1 What Languages Do You Speak?

_____

_____

_____

_____

_____

_____

_____

_____

Unit 2 Don't Worry, Be Happy

_____

_____

_____

_____

_____

_____

_____

_____

Unit 3 Home and Family

_____

_____

_____

_____

_____

_____

_____

_____

_____

Unit 4 Winning and Losing

_____

_____

_____

_____

_____

_____

_____

_____

_____

Unit 5 Healing Power

_____

_____

_____

_____

_____

_____

_____

_____

Unit 6 Crime

_____

_____

_____

_____

_____

_____

_____

_____

_____

Unit 7 The Universe and Beyond

_____

_____

_____

_____

_____

_____

_____

_____

_____

Unit 8 Business Savvy

_____

_____

_____

_____

_____

_____

_____

_____

_____